FIRST
FACTS
ABOUT
**THE
STATES**

Published by Blackbirch Press, Inc.
260 Amity Road
Woodbridge, CT 06525

© 1996 Blackbirch Press, Inc.
First Edition

Printed in Hong Kong

10 9 8 7 6 5 4 3 2

Photo Credits

Cover photos (clockwise from top): Mt. Rushmore, Black Hills, South Dakota: South Dakota Tourism; Grand Tetons, Grand Tetons National Park, Wyoming: Wyoming Division of Tourism; Independence Hall, Philadelphia, Pennsylvania: Pennsylvania Office of Travel Marketing; The Alamo, San Antonio, Texas: Texas Department of Transportation; The Statue of Liberty, New York: ©Blackbirch Press, Inc.; Magnolia blossom: Courtesy of the Mississippi Tourism Department; California State flag: ©Blackbirch Press, Inc.

Contents photos (top to bottom): Page 4: Las Vegas, Nevada: ©Henry Kaiser, Leo de Wys, Inc.; Hilton Head, South Carolina: Fridmar Damm/Leo de Wys, Inc.; Mount Rushmore, Black Hills, South Dakota: South Dakota Tourism. Page 5: San Francisco, California: ©Steve Vidler/Leo de Wys, Inc.; The Gateway Arch, St. Louis, Missouri: ©Steve Vidler/Leo de Wys, Inc.; Florida Department of Commerce, Division of Tourism.

Pages 6–7: Alabama Division of Tourism and Travel; pages 8–9: Alaska Division of Tourism; pages 10, 81 (top): Richard Frear/National Park Service; page 11: ©Rainer Hackenberg/Arizona Office of Tourism; page 12: ©Bob Krist/Leo de Wys, Inc.; page 13: Arkansas Department of Parks and Tourism; pages 14, 16, 54, 66: ©Steve Vidler/Leo de Wys, Inc.; page 15: Robert Holmes/California Office of Tourism; page 17 (top): ©Bob Thomason/Leo de Wys, Inc.; page 17 (bottom): ©David Lissy/Leo de Wys, Inc.; page 18: ©Grace Schaub/Leo de Wys, Inc.; page 19: Connecticut Department of Economic Development; pages 20–21: Delaware Tourism Office; pages 22, 84: Fridmar Damm/Leo de Wys, Inc.; page 23: Florida Department of Commerce, Division of Tourism; pages 24–25: Georgia Department of Industry, Trade and Tourism; pages 26, 99 (top): ©Robert Knight/Leo de Wys, Inc.; pages 27 (top): ©Leo de Wys, Inc.; pages 27 (bottom), 32: ©Everett C. Johnson/Leo de Wys, Inc.; page 28: ©J. Blank/Leo de Wys, Inc.; page 29 (top): ©Allan Preston/Leo de Wys, Inc.; page 29 (bottom): ©Casimir/Leo de Wys, Inc.; page 30: ©Vic Bider/Leo de Wys, Inc.; page 31: ©Peter Pearson/Leo de Wys, Inc.; page 33: Indiana Department of Tourism; pages 34–35: Iowa Division of Tourism; page 36: ©Ed Lallo/Liaison International; page 37: Kansas Division of Tourism and Travel; pages 38–39: Kentucky Department of Travel Development; page 40: ©J. Messerschmidt/Leo de Wys, Inc.; page 41: Louisiana Office of Tourism; pages 42–43: Maine Office of Tourism; page 44: ©Ron Solomon/Leo de Wys, Inc.; page 45: Maryland Office of Tourism and Development; pages 47 (top), 60, 62, 104: ©Henryk Kaiser/Leo de Wys, Inc.; page 47 (bottom): Vincent Serbin/Leo de Wys, Inc.; pages 48–49: Courtesy Michigan Travel Bureau; pages 50–51: ©Minnesota Office of Tourism; pages 52–53: Photos courtesy of the Mississippi Tourism Department; page 55: Permission granted by the Missouri Division of Tourism; pages 56–57 (top): Travel Montana; page 57 (bottom): Travel Montana/D. Broussard; pages 58–59: Nebraska Department of Economic Development; page 61: Nevada Commission on Tourism; page 63: New Hampshire Office of Travel and Tourism Development; pages 64–65: Courtesy New Jersey Division of Travel and Tourism; pages 46, 67: ©Vladpans/Leo de Wys, Inc.; pages 68, 69 (bottom): New York State Department of Economic Development; pages 69 (top), 106, 107 (top): ©Blackbirch Press, Inc.; pages 70–71: North Carolina Division of Travel and Tourism; pages 72–73: North Dakota Tourism Department; pages 74–75: Greater Columbus Convention and Visitors Bureau; pages 76–77: Fred W. Marvel/Oklahoma Tourism and Recreation Department; pages 78–79: Oregon Tourism Division; page 80: ©Sylvain Grandadam/Tony Stone Images; page 81 (bottom): Pennsylvania Office of Travel Marketing; page 82: ©Leonard Harris/Leo de Wys, Inc.; page 83: Rhode Island Tourism Division; page 85: South Carolina Department of Parks, Recreation and Tourism; pages 86–87: Photos by South Dakota Tourism; pages 88–89: Tennessee Tourist Development; pages 90–91: Texas Department of Transportation; pages 92–93: Utah Travel Council; pages 94–95: Vermont Department of Travel and Tourism; pages 96–97: Virginia Division of Tourism; page 98: ©Mike Howell/Leo de Wys, Inc.; page 99 (bottom): ©Edward Thomas/Leo de Wys, Inc.; pages 100–101: Steve Shaluta, Jr./West Virginia Division of Tourism; pages 102–103: Wisconsin Division of Tourism; page 105: Wyoming Division of Tourism; page 107 (bottom): William Clark/National Park Service; pages 108, 109 (top): Photo by Bob Krist for the Puerto Rico Tourism Co.; page 109 (bottom): Guam Visitors Bureau.

Maps by Blackbirch Graphics, Inc.

Library of Congress Cataloging-in-Publication Data

Stienecker, David L.
    First facts about the states / by David L. Stienecker
       p.   cm. — (First facts)
    Includes bibliographical references (p.) and index.
    Summary: Gives the birds, flowers, and trees for all fifty states, as well as important dates in each state's history.
    ISBN 1-56711-166-1 (alk. paper)
      1. United States—Miscellanea—Juvenile literature. [1. United States—Miscellanea.]
I. Title. II. Series: First facts about . . .
(Woodbridge, Conn.)
E180.S76   1996
973—dc20
                                                  95-34384
                                                     CIP
                                                     AC

FIRST
FACTS
ABOUT

THE
STATES

★ ★ ★

by

David L. Stienecker

BLACKBIRCH PRESS, INC.
WOODBRIDGE, CONNECTICUT

Contents

ALABAMA

HEART OF DIXIE; CAMELLIA STATE

Fishing on a lake in Madison County.

State bird:	Yellowhammer (flicker)
State flower:	Camellia
State tree:	Southern pine
Name:	Alabama was named after a tribe of Native Americans who once lived in the area. They called themselves the Alibamu, perhaps from words meaning "to clear the vegetation"
Motto:	*Audemus jura nostra defendere* ("We dare defend our rights")
Song:	"Alabama." Words by Julia S. Tutwiler; music by Edna Goeckel Gussen
State capital:	Montgomery
Population:	4,186,806 (1993); ranked 22nd
Total area:	51,705 square miles; ranked 31st
Abbreviation:	Ala. (traditional); AL (postal)

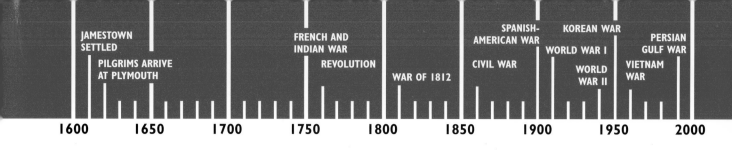

JAMESTOWN
SETTLED

PILGRIMS ARRIVE
AT PLYMOUTH

FRENCH AND
INDIAN WAR

REVOLUTION

WAR OF 1812

SPANISH-
AMERICAN WAR

CIVIL WAR

KOREAN WAR

WORLD WAR I

WORLD
WAR II

PERSIAN
GULF WAR

VIETNAM
WAR

1600   1650   1700   1750   1800   1850   1900   1950   2000

Alabama is in the heart of the Deep South. During the Civil War, Alabama was the center of the Southern Confederacy. Almost a century later, many important events in the modern civil rights movement took place there.

Most of northern Alabama is covered by forested hills. As you move south, the hills give way to rolling grasslands and rich farmland. The Mobile Delta, bordering on the Gulf of Mexico, has many swamps and bayous (swampy streams). Mobile Bay is lined with sandy beaches, while the city of Mobile is a busy seaport.

Alabama's mild climate and rich soil make it an important farming state. Its major crops include peanuts, cotton, soybeans, wheat, and pecans. Because of its vast forests, Alabama also produces much lumber. The state's industries include steel production and electronics manufacturing. Huntsville has become known as Rocket City, U.S.A., because many important rockets and space vehicles have been developed there.

Below: U.S. Space and Rocket Center, in Huntsville.
Bottom: Horton Mill Covered Bridge, Oneonta.

IMPORTANT DATES

• **1540:** The Spanish explorer Hernando de Soto leads an expedition into what is now the Alabama region.
• **1702:** The French establish Fort Louis, the first permanent settlement in Alabama.
• **1763:** France gives the Alabama region to Great Britain.
• **1783:** Great Britain gives the United States much of present-day Alabama. It gives the Mobile region to Spain.
• **1813:** The United States captures Mobile Bay from Spain.
• **1819:** On December 14, Alabama becomes the 22nd state.
• **1846:** The state capital is moved to Montgomery.
• **1861:** Alabama joins the Confederacy early on in the Civil War.
• **1955:** Rosa Parks, an African American, refuses to give up her seat to a white bus passenger, sparking the civil rights movement.
• **1965:** Martin Luther King, Jr., leads a march from Selma to Montgomery to protest racial discrimination.

OF SPECIAL INTEREST

• Russell Cave near Bridgeport is believed to have been the home of cliff-dwelling Native Americans 8,000 to 9,000 years ago.
• The first electric streetcars in the United States began operating in Montgomery in 1886.
• The boll weevil, an insect, destroyed Alabama's cotton crop in 1910. The state's farmers, who had depended on cotton, then learned to grow a wide variety of other crops.

ALASKA

THE LAST FRONTIER

Wood-carved totems of the Klawok.

State bird:	Willow ptarmigan
State flower:	Forget-me-not
State tree:	Sitka spruce
Name:	The name *Alaska* comes from the Aleut word *alakshak*, which means "great land" or "mainland"
Motto:	"North to the future"
Song:	"Alaska's Flag." Words by Marie Drake; music by Elinor Dusenbury
State capital:	Juneau
Population:	599,151 (1993); ranked 48th
Total area:	591,004 square miles, ranked 1st
Abbreviation:	AK (postal)

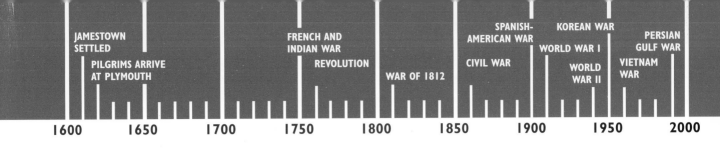

JAMESTOWN SETTLED		FRENCH AND INDIAN WAR			SPANISH-AMERICAN WAR	KOREAN WAR	PERSIAN GULF WAR

PILGRIMS ARRIVE AT PLYMOUTH

REVOLUTION

WORLD WAR I

CIVIL WAR

WAR OF 1812

WORLD WAR II

VIETNAM WAR

1600   1650   1700   1750   1800   1850   1900   1950   2000

Alaska is the largest state—almost a fifth as large as all the rest of the United States combined, and more than twice the size of Texas, the second-largest state. Alaska is also a land of spectacular natural beauty, with towering mountains, deep canyons, vast glaciers, and abundant wildlife.

Almost a third of Alaska lies north of the Arctic Circle. Much of this land is a vast wilderness of frozen tundra, ice fields, lakes, forests, and mountains. Temperatures vary widely from region to region and season to season. They range from averages of -20°F to 30°F in the winter, 56°F to 90°F in the summer. In the summer, the sun shines about 20 hours a day. At Point Barrow, the northernmost point in Alaska, the sun never sets from May 10 to August 2.

Alaska's native peoples learned long ago how to live in these harsh conditions. They depended on hunting to survive. Today, important industries in Alaska include commercial fishing, natural gas, and tourism.

IMPORTANT DATES
• **1741:** Captain Vitus Bering of Denmark, sailing for Russia, lands on Alaskan islands.
• **1784:** Russian settlers establish a fur-trading station, the first white settlement in Alaska, on Kodiak Island.
• **1867:** The United States buys Alaska from Russia for $7.2 million.
• **1896:** Gold is discovered in Yukon, northwest Canada, setting off the Klondike and Alaska gold rushes.
• **1959:** On January 3, Alaska becomes the 49th state.
• **1968:** Large oil deposits are discovered near Prudhoe Bay.
• **1977:** The 789-mile-long Trans-Alaska oil pipeline is completed.
• **1980:** Nearly a fourth of Alaska's land is set aside as part of the National Park System.
• **1989:** The oil tanker *Exxon Valdez* runs aground in Prince William Sound, producing the biggest oil spill in U.S. history.

OF SPECIAL INTEREST
• Alaska has more coastline than any other state in the nation.
• More bald eagles gather along the Chilkat River just north of Haines than at any other place in the world.
• Malaspina Glacier, west of Yakutat Bay, is North America's largest glacier. It is larger than the state of Rhode Island.
• Mount McKinley, in central Alaska, is the highest mountain in North America. It rises 20,320 feet above sea level.

Top: Northern lights, in Fairbanks.
Bottom: Mendenhall Glacier, near Juneau.

9

ARIZONA

GRAND CANYON STATE

The Grand Canyon.

State bird: Cactus wren
State flower: Blossom of the saguaro cactus
State tree: Paloverde
Name: The name *Arizona* comes from a Native-American word. It may be the Spanish version of the Papago word *Arizonac* or the Pima word *Arizuma*, meaning "little spring"
Motto: *Ditat Deus* ("God enriches")
Song: "Arizona." Words by Margaret Rowe Clifford; music by Maurice Blumenthal
State capital: Phoenix
Population: 3,936,142 (1993); ranked 23rd
Total area: 114,000 square miles; ranked 6th
Abbreviation: Ariz. (traditional); AZ (postal)

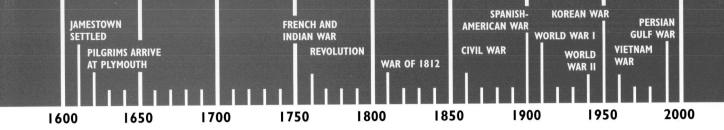

JAMESTOWN
SETTLED

PILGRIMS ARRIVE
AT PLYMOUTH

FRENCH AND
INDIAN WAR

REVOLUTION

WAR OF 1812

SPANISH-
AMERICAN WAR

CIVIL WAR

KOREAN WAR

WORLD WAR I

WORLD
WAR II

PERSIAN
GULF WAR

VIETNAM
WAR

1600   1650   1700   1750   1800   1850   1900   1950   2000

Arizona is home to one of America's most famous natural features—the Grand Canyon. Millions of people travel to Arizona each year to visit this and other natural wonders, such as the Painted Desert, the Petrified Forest, and the Sonoran (or Gila) Desert.

Much of Arizona is desert. The desert summers are very hot and dry, but the winters are warm and pleasant. Arizona's climate attracts so many people that the state has become one of the nation's fastest-growing areas. More than half the state is covered with mountains and plateaus. These higher, cooler areas have the largest ponderosa pine forests in the United States.

Huge dams trap the waters of the Colorado and other major rivers for use by Arizona's cities and farms. Irrigation has turned desert into productive cropland, with cotton, vegetables, and sorghum among the chief crops. Cattle and sheep are raised in the cooler regions of the state. Major industries include electronics and the mining of copper, gold, and silver.

IMPORTANT DATES

• **1540:** The Spanish explorer Francisco Vásquez de Coronado visits parts of what is now the Arizona region.

• **1692:** Father Eusebio Kino works with members of the Pima tribe and founds a mission.

• **1776:** The Spanish establish a fort at Tucson.

• **1848:** After the Mexican War, Mexico turns over most of present-day Arizona to the United States.

• **1853:** The Gadsden Purchase from Mexico adds the rest of present-day Arizona.

• **1886:** Apache leader Geronimo surrenders, ending the Indian Wars.

• **1912:** On February 14, Arizona becomes the 48th state.

• **1919:** Grand Canyon National Park is established.

OF SPECIAL INTEREST

• The town of Oraibi is believed to be the oldest inhabited village in the United States. It was built by people of the Hopi tribe in the 1100s.

• On July 4, 1888, the first official rodeo was held, at Prescott.

• The planet Pluto was discovered from Lowell Observatory in Flagstaff in 1930.

• Tucson is known as the Astronomy Capital of the World. There are more telescopes in this area than anyplace else.

• Kitt Peak National Observatory near Tucson has the largest solar telescope in the world.

Top: Window Rock.
Bottom: A rodeo in Page.

ARKANSAS

LAND OF OPPORTUNITY

State bird: Mockingbird
State flower: Apple blossom
State tree: Pine tree
Name: The name *Arkansas* comes from the Native-American word *Quapaw,* which means "downstream people"
Motto: *Regnat populus* ("The people rule")
Song: "Arkansas." Words and music by Eva Ware Barnett
State capital: Little Rock
Population: 2,424,418 (1993); ranked 33rd
Total area: 53,187 square miles; ranked 29th
Abbreviation: Ark. (traditional); AR (postal)

Two hikers stop for a breathtaking view atop Whittaker Point, in the Ozark Mountains.

JAMESTOWN SETTLED		FRENCH AND INDIAN WAR				SPANISH-AMERICAN WAR	KOREAN WAR		PERSIAN GULF WAR
PILGRIMS ARRIVE AT PLYMOUTH			REVOLUTION				WORLD WAR I		
				WAR OF 1812		CIVIL WAR		WORLD WAR II	VIETNAM WAR

| 1600 | 1650 | 1700 | 1750 | 1800 | 1850 | 1900 | 1950 | 2000 |

State Capitol, in Little Rock.

Arkansas is a land of beautiful mountains and valleys, thick forests, flat plains, and rolling prairies. It is famous for its many natural springs. Some people believe that the spring waters can help cure certain ailments. Mammoth Spring is one of the largest natural springs in the world. Hot Springs is famous as a health center.

The Ozark and Quachita Mountains, in northern and western Arkansas, are called the Highlands. This is a region of small towns and farms, including poultry farms. The flat plains and rolling prairies in the southern and eastern regions of the state are called the Lowlands. Farms here are larger, and more people live in this part of the state. Arkansas has a warm, moist climate. The summers are warm-to-hot, and the winters are cool.

Food processing is among Arkansas's leading industries. The state also produces bauxite, an ore from which aluminum is made. Its many forests make lumber and wood products important industries, too. Arkansas's rich farmland produces many crops, including rice, cotton, and soybeans.

IMPORTANT DATES
- **1541-1542:** Hernando de Soto of Spain explores the region.
- **1682:** Sieur de La Salle claims the Mississippi Valley for France.
- **1803:** The United States acquires Arkansas from France as part of the Louisiana Purchase.
- **1836:** On June 15, Arkansas becomes the 25th state.
- **1861:** Arkansas joins the Confederacy in the Civil War.
- **1957:** The National Guard helps enforce school integration at Little Rock's Central High School.
- **1992:** Arkansas governor Bill Clinton is elected president of the United States.

OF SPECIAL INTEREST
- The Norfork National Fish Hatchery in Mountain Home is the largest federal trout hatchery in the United States. Each year, some 2 million trout are raised from eggs here.
- Hot Springs is the only U.S. city with almost all of a national park within its limits.
- The Crater of Diamonds, near Murfreesboro, is the only diamond mine in the United States.

Apple blossom.

13

CALIFORNIA

GOLDEN STATE

A cable car climbs one of San Francisco's many steep hills.

State bird: California valley quail

State flower: Golden poppy

State tree: California redwood

Name: California was named after an imaginary island in a popular Spanish story written in the early 1500s

Motto: *Eureka* ("I have found it")

Song: "I Love You, California." Words by F. B. Silverwood; music by A. F. Frankenstein

State capital: Sacramento

Population: 31,210,750 (1993); ranked 1st

Total area: 158,706 square miles; ranked 3rd

Abbreviation: Calif. (traditional); CA (postal)

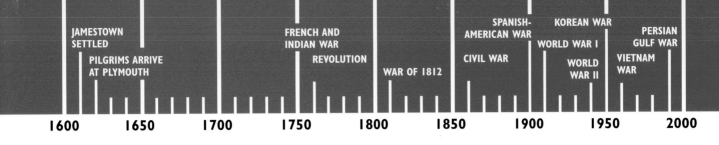

| JAMESTOWN SETTLED | PILGRIMS ARRIVE AT PLYMOUTH | FRENCH AND INDIAN WAR REVOLUTION | WAR OF 1812 | SPANISH-AMERICAN WAR CIVIL WAR | KOREAN WAR WORLD WAR I WORLD WAR II | PERSIAN GULF WAR VIETNAM WAR |

1600   1650   1700   1750   1800   1850   1900   1950   2000

Ever since gold was found there in 1848, California has been a magnet for fortune-seekers. Today, more people live in California than in any other state. Millions of people also visit each year. They go to enjoy California's natural beauty—its beautiful beaches, towering mountains, and majestic redwood forests. They are also lured by attractions such as Disneyland, in Anaheim, Hollywood, in Los Angeles, and scenic cities such as San Francisco.

The California coastline stretches 840 miles along the Pacific Ocean. The Sierra Nevada Mountains rise near California's eastern border. Vast redwood forests cover the coastal areas of the north, and barren deserts extend across the southeast.

California's Central Valley, about 400 miles long, is the nation's leading agricultural area. Its fertile soil produces a wide variety of fruits, nuts, and vegetables as well as cotton, rice, and wheat. California is an important national and world center for the defense, aerospace, and electronics industries. Hollywood is the entertainment capital of the world.

IMPORTANT DATES

• **1542:** Juan Rodríguez Cabrillo explores San Diego Bay.
• **1769:** Junípero Serra founds the first Franciscan mission in California, near present-day San Diego.
• **1846:** U.S. forces take California during the Mexican War.
• **1847:** California becomes a U.S. territory.
• **1848:** James W. Marshall discovers gold at Sutter's Mill.
• **1850:** On September 9, California becomes the 31st state.
• **1906:** A major earthquake and fire destroy most of San Francisco.
• **1963:** California becomes the state with the largest population.
• **1989:** The San Francisco Bay Area is rocked by a massive earthquake.
• **1994:** A severe earthquake strikes Los Angeles.

OF SPECIAL INTEREST

• The highest temperature ever recorded in the United States (134°F) was at Death Valley on July 10, 1913.
• Death Valley is the lowest point in the United States, 282 feet below sea level.
• The world's tallest known tree is in the Tall Trees Grove in Redwood National Park. It is 368 feet tall.
• The first cable-car system began operation in San Francisco in 1873.

Top: The lighthouse at Pigeon Point.
Bottom: Rose Bowl parade, in Pasadena.

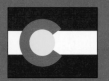

COLORADO

CENTENNIAL STATE

Cliff palace dwellings of Mesa Verde National Park.

State bird: Lark bunting
State flower: Rocky Mountain columbine
State tree: Blue spruce
Name: *Colorado* is a Spanish word that means "colored" or "reddish." The name was first given to the Colorado River because it flows through red stone canyons. The state took its name from the river
Motto: *Nil sine numine* ("Nothing without providence")
Song: "Where the Columbines Grow." Words and music by A. J. Flynn
State capital: Denver
Population: 3,565,959 (1993); ranked 26th
Total area: 104,091 square miles; ranked 8th
Abbreviation: Colo. (traditional); CO (postal)

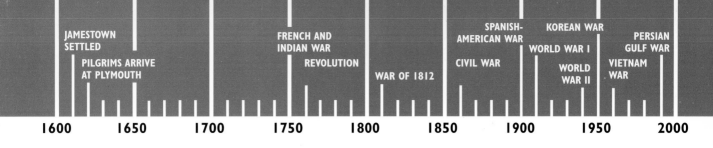

JAMESTOWN SETTLED		FRENCH AND INDIAN WAR				SPANISH-AMERICAN WAR	KOREAN WAR	
PILGRIMS ARRIVE AT PLYMOUTH		REVOLUTION			CIVIL WAR	WORLD WAR I	PERSIAN GULF WAR
			WAR OF 1812			WORLD WAR II	VIETNAM WAR

| 1600 | 1650 | 1700 | 1750 | 1800 | 1850 | 1900 | 1950 | 2000 |

Colorado is one of the Rocky Mountain states. The Rockies' natural beauty and pleasant climate attract millions of summer vacationers. In winter, the snow-covered slopes of Aspen, Vail, and other resorts draw skiers from all over the world.

More than half of Colorado is mountainous, making it the highest of all states. Over 800 peaks rise above 10,000 feet, and more than 50 of these are at least 14,000 feet high. The eastern third of the state is part of the Great Plains region. The plains gradually slope upward from east to west until they meet the base of the Rocky Mountains.

About half of Colorado's land is used for grazing cattle and sheep. Farms produce abundant crops of

wheat, corn, hay, and sugar beets. Colorado is also rich in mineral re-sources. The state's most important min-eral product is petroleum. Colorado mine production includes gold, zinc, lead, and molybdenum.

IMPORTANT DATES

• **1803:** The United States buys present-day eastern Colorado from the French in the Louisiana Purchase.
• **1806:** Zebulon Pike discovers the peak that was later named for him.
• **1848:** Mexico gives up part of Colorado to the United States after the Mexican War.
• **1859:** The Pikes Peak gold rush attracts thousands of prospectors and settlers.
• **1876:** On August 1, Colorado becomes the 38th state.
• **1915:** Rocky Mountain National Park is created.
• **1958:** The Air Force Academy opens near Colorado Springs.
• **1965:** The North American Air Defense Command opens its combat operations center inside Cheyenne Mountain.

OF SPECIAL INTEREST

• Colorado is the highest state. Its average altitude is about 6,800 feet above sea level.
• The largest silver nugget ever found in North America was discovered in Aspen in 1894. It weighed 1,840 pounds.
• Fossil remains of dinosaurs have been discovered at Dinosaur National Monument, in Colorado and Utah.
• The world's highest suspension bridge spans Royal Gorge, near Canon City.
• Hundreds of years ago, Native Americans built cliff dwellings at what is now Mesa Verde National Park near Cortez.

Top: A beautiful view at Snowmass, near Aspen.
Bottom: The Royal Gorge Bridge, near Canon City.

17

CONNECTICUT

CONSTITUTION STATE; NUTMEG STATE

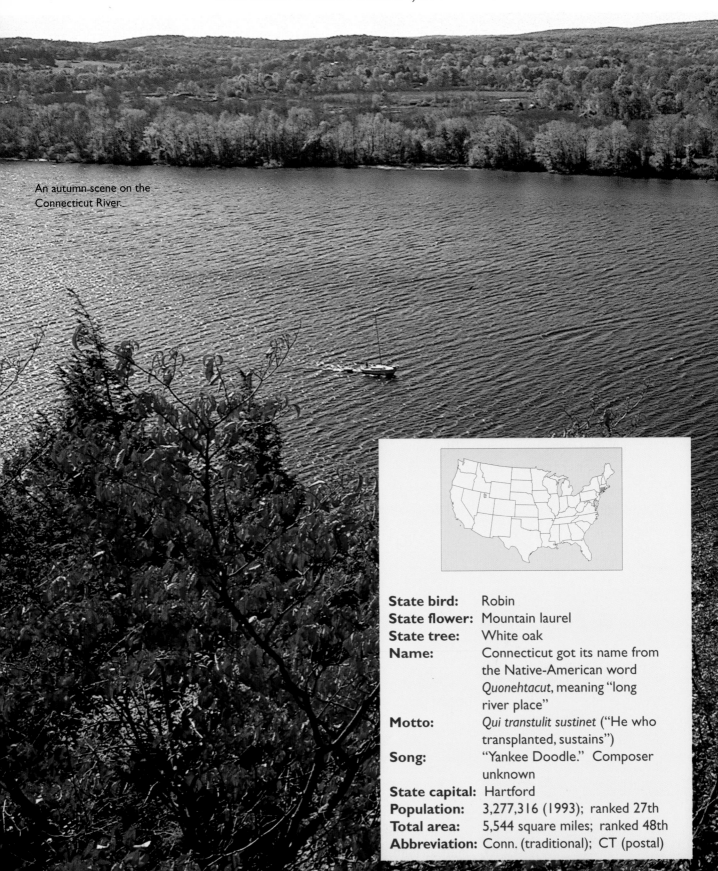

An autumn scene on the Connecticut River.

State bird:	Robin
State flower:	Mountain laurel
State tree:	White oak
Name:	Connecticut got its name from the Native-American word *Quonehtacut*, meaning "long river place"
Motto:	*Qui transtulit sustinet* ("He who transplanted, sustains")
Song:	"Yankee Doodle." Composer unknown
State capital:	Hartford
Population:	3,277,316 (1993); ranked 27th
Total area:	5,544 square miles; ranked 48th
Abbreviation:	Conn. (traditional); CT (postal)

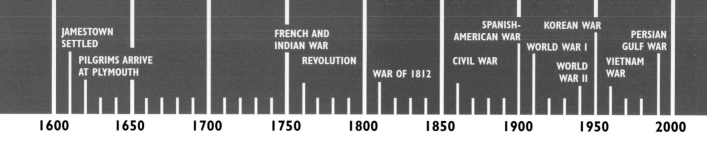

JAMESTOWN SETTLED		FRENCH AND INDIAN WAR				SPANISH-AMERICAN WAR	KOREAN WAR		PERSIAN GULF WAR
PILGRIMS ARRIVE AT PLYMOUTH		REVOLUTION					WORLD WAR I		VIETNAM WAR
				WAR OF 1812		CIVIL WAR		WORLD WAR II	

| 1600 | 1650 | 1700 | 1750 | 1800 | 1850 | 1900 | 1950 | 2000 |

Connecticut is the southernmost of the New England states. Although it is the third-smallest state, it has a rich history. Connecticut was one of the original Thirteen Colonies. And the first constitution in America, a document called the Fundamental Orders, was written there more than 350 years ago.

Rolling hills, valleys, rivers, lakes, and waterfalls make Connecticut a beautiful land. The Connecticut River cuts through the center of the state and flows into Long Island Sound. The sound is Connecticut's outlet to the Atlantic Ocean and provides it with more than 250 miles of coastline.

Rushing streams provided waterpower for industry in Connecticut's early days. The state was known throughout the world for its brass, clocks, guns, and other products. Today, it is a leading manufacturer of helicopters, jet engines, and submarines. Connecticut is also a center of the insurance industry. Connecticut farms raise dairy cattle and crops such as sweet corn.

IMPORTANT DATES
• **1614:** Adriaen Block, a Dutch navigator, explores the Connecticut region.
• **1633:** The first English colonists settle at Windsor.
• **1701:** Collegiate School, later Yale University, is founded in New Haven.
• **1788:** On January 9, Connecticut becomes the fifth state.
• **1932:** New London becomes the home of the U.S. Coast Guard Academy.
• **1954:** The first atomic submarine, the U.S.S. *Nautilus*, is launched from Groton.
• **1979:** Connecticut passes a law banning construction of new nuclear power plants.
• **1983:** The Pequot Indians of eastern Connecticut win land claims against the state.
• **1995:** New Haven hosts the International Special Olympics.

OF SPECIAL INTEREST
• *The Hartford Courant* has been published longer than any other daily newspaper in the United States. *The Courant* began in 1764.
• The nation's first law school was founded at Litchfield in 1774.
• The first telephone exchange in the world opened in New Haven on January 28, 1878.
• The first cookbook written by an American was published in Hartford in 1796. It was *American Cookery* by Amelia Simmons.
• The football tackling dummy was invented in 1889 at Yale University.

Top: The New England Air Museum, in Windsor Locks.
Bottom: The old whaling ships at Mystic Seaport, in Mystic.

DELAWARE

FIRST STATE; DIAMOND STATE

Tall, modern buildings make up the skyline in Wilmington.

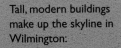

State bird:	Blue hen chicken
State flower:	Peach blossom
State tree:	American holly
Name:	Delaware was named for Lord De La Warr, an early governor of Virginia. The name was given first to the Delaware River, then to the state
Motto:	"Liberty and independence"
Song:	"Our Delaware." Words by George B. Hynson; music by William M. S. Brown
State capital:	Dover
Population:	700,269 (1993); ranked 46th
Total area:	2,489 square miles; ranked 49th
Abbreviation:	Del. (traditional); DE (postal)

JAMESTOWN SETTLED		FRENCH AND INDIAN WAR			SPANISH-AMERICAN WAR	KOREAN WAR	PERSIAN GULF WAR
PILGRIMS ARRIVE AT PLYMOUTH		REVOLUTION		CIVIL WAR	WORLD WAR I	VIETNAM WAR	
			WAR OF 1812		WORLD WAR II		

| 1600 | 1650 | 1700 | 1750 | 1800 | 1850 | 1900 | 1950 | 2000 |

Delaware earned its nickname by becoming the first state to adopt the Constitution. It is the second-smallest state, and only four other states have fewer people. Delaware is located close to many of the nation's largest cities, including Baltimore, New York City, Philadelphia, and Washington, D.C., making it an important trading center.

Most of Delaware is covered by flat, fertile land, and about half the state is farmland. Rolling hills and valleys cover the northern tip of the state, a region known as the Piedmont. Delaware's Atlantic coastline provides dune-covered beaches that are popular summer vacation spots.

Chemicals are Delaware's most important product. Chemical companies also produce plastics, synthetic fibers, dyes, and paints. Poultry is the leading farm product, and soybeans are the chief crop. Other major crops include corn, potatoes, and mushrooms. Leather making has been an important industry since 1732.

IMPORTANT DATES

• **1609:** Henry Hudson explores Delaware Bay and the Delaware River.
• **1638:** Swedish colonists found Fort Christina, Delaware's first permanent European settlement.
• **1664:** Delaware comes under English rule.
• **1682:** William Penn takes over the Delaware counties.
• **1763-1768:** Charles Mason and Jeremiah Dixon survey the Delaware boundaries.
• **1787:** On December 7, Delaware becomes the first state.
• **1802:** E. I. du Pont opens a gunpowder mill at Wilmington, founding the Du Pont Company.
• **1834:** The University of Delaware is founded at Newark.
• **1937:** Wallace H. Carothers of the Du Pont Company in Wilmington invents nylon.
• **1971:** The Coastal Zone Act prohibits the development of heavy industry along the state's shoreline.

OF SPECIAL INTEREST

• Swedish immigrants who settled in southern Delaware were the first to introduce log cabins to North America.
• The first iron, propeller-driven seagoing ship built in the United States was launched at Wilmington in 1844.
• The first beauty pageant in the United States was held at Rehoboth Beach in 1880.

Top: Rehoboth Beach.
Bottom: One of Delaware's many historic homes, at New Castle.

21

FLORIDA

SUNSHINE STATE

A marsh in the Everglades.

State bird:	Mockingbird
State flower:	Orange blossom
State tree:	Sabal palm
Name:	Juan Ponce de León gave Florida its name. *Florida* is a Spanish word meaning "full of flowers"
Motto:	"In God we trust"
Song:	"Swanee River." Words and music by Stephen Foster
State capital:	Tallahassee
Population:	13,678,914 (1993); ranked 4th
Total area:	65,756 square miles; ranked 22nd
Abbreviation:	Fla. (traditional); FL (postal)

JAMESTOWN SETTLED		FRENCH AND INDIAN WAR			SPANISH-AMERICAN WAR	KOREAN WAR	PERSIAN GULF WAR
PILGRIMS ARRIVE AT PLYMOUTH		REVOLUTION			WORLD WAR I		
			WAR OF 1812	CIVIL WAR		WORLD WAR II	VIETNAM WAR

1600   1650   1700   1750   1800   1850   1900   1950   2000

A sunny beach near Miami.

Approximately 40 million vacationers visit the state of Florida each year. They go for the sunny, warm climate and for Florida's many other attractions. Some of the most popular are Walt Disney World, Sea World, Everglades National Park, and the Kennedy Space Center at Cape Canaveral.

Florida juts more than 350 miles into the Atlantic Ocean and is surrounded by water on three sides. Its coastline is longer than that of any other state except Alaska. It provides another of Florida's main attractions—its beautiful, sandy beaches.

About two thirds of the oranges and three fourths of the grapefruits used in the nation come from Florida. Sugarcane is another chief crop. Florida also ranks first in the production of house plants. Livestock production is an important part of the economy. Among Florida's other major industries is the manufacture of aerospace and aircraft equipment.

IMPORTANT DATES
• **1513:** Juan Ponce de León claims the Florida region for Spain.
• **1565:** St. Augustine becomes the first permanent European settlement in what is now the United States.
• **1821:** Florida comes under U.S. control after being given up by Spain.
• **1835:** The Seminole War breaks out between U.S. forces and native peoples, the Seminoles.
• **1845:** On March 3, Florida becomes the 27th state.
• **1861:** Florida joins the Confederacy in the Civil War.
• **1962:** The first U.S. manned space flights are launched from Cape Canaveral.
• **1971:** Disney World opens near Orlando.
• **1992:** Hurricane Andrew damages Florida's agriculture and economy.

OF SPECIAL INTEREST
• St. Augustine is the oldest city in the nation.
• In 1903, President Theodore Roosevelt established the first federal wildlife refuge in the United States at Pelican Island.
• The Everglades is a vast watery wilderness in southern Florida. Much of it is protected in parks and preserves.
• Since the 1960s, thousands of refugees from Cuba and other Latin American countries have settled in Florida.
• *Apollo 11* was launched from Cape Canaveral on July 16, 1969, carrying astronauts to the moon for the first time.
• The Florida Keys are a series of small coral islands that extend more than 150 miles from Florida's southernmost tip.

23

GEORGIA

EMPIRE STATE OF THE SOUTH; PEACH STATE

State bird: Brown thrasher
State flower: Cherokee rose
State tree: Live oak
Name: Georgia was named for King George II of England
Motto: "Wisdom, justice, and moderation"
Song: "Georgia on My Mind." Words by Stuart Gorrell; music by Hoagy Carmichael
State capital: Atlanta
Population: 6,917,140 (1993); ranked 11th
Total area: 59,441 square miles; ranked 24th
Abbreviation: Ga. (traditional); GA (postal)

Peachtree Center, in downtown Atlanta.

JAMESTOWN SETTLED		FRENCH AND INDIAN WAR				SPANISH-AMERICAN WAR	KOREAN WAR	
	PILGRIMS ARRIVE AT PLYMOUTH		REVOLUTION			CIVIL WAR	WORLD WAR I	PERSIAN GULF WAR
				WAR OF 1812			WORLD WAR II	VIETNAM WAR

1600	1650	1700	1750	1800	1850	1900	1950	2000

Georgia is the largest state east of the Mississippi River. It is almost the size of all the New England states combined. The capital of Georgia, Atlanta, is the manufacturing and business center of the Southeast. The state's natural beauty has inspired many songs and stories.

The pine-covered Blue Ridge Mountains stretch across the northern part of Georgia. West of these mountains lies the fertile Appalachian Valley. Flat coastal plains extend eastward to the Atlantic Ocean and form the southern half of the state. This area includes the vast Okefenokee National Wildlife Refuge. Most of the state has a mild climate, with warm, humid summers, and cool, short winters.

Cotton and cotton cloth were once Georgia's main products, and the state still produces textiles. Today, however, Georgia farmers also grow peanuts, soybeans, pecans, tobacco, corn, and wheat—no other state grows more peanuts. Georgia's famous peaches are grown mostly along the Atlantic coast. The state is also one of the nation's leading producers of forest products. Marble and granite are quarried in northern Georgia; Georgia marble was used to build the Lincoln Memorial in Washington, D.C.

IMPORTANT DATES

- **1540:** The Spanish explorer Hernando de Soto marches through part of present-day Georgia.
- **1733:** James Oglethorpe brings the first English settlers to Georgia and founds Savannah.
- **1788:** On January 2, Georgia becomes the 4th state.
- **1838:** Cherokees are forced to leave their lands in Georgia.
- **1861:** Georgia joins the Confederacy in the Civil War.
- **1948:** Georgia is the first state to allow 18-year-olds to vote.
- **1980:** The world's largest airport terminal opens in Atlanta.
- **1996:** Atlanta is the site of the Summer Olympic Games.

OF SPECIAL INTEREST

- Eli Whitney invented the cotton gin near Savannah in 1793. It helped make cotton the leading crop of the South.
- The first steamship to cross the Atlantic Ocean sailed from Savannah for Liverpool, England, in 1819.
- *The Cherokee Phoenix* was the first known newspaper in the United States to use a Native-American language. It was first printed in New Echota in 1828.
- The Girl Scouts of the U.S.A. organization was founded by Jullette Gordon Low in Savannah on March 12, 1912.

Top: Cherokee roses in bloom.
Bottom: Cumberland Island National Seashore.

HAWAII

THE ALOHA STATE

The Honolulu skyline at dusk.

State bird:	Nene (Hawaiian goose)
State flower:	Yellow hibiscus
State tree:	Kukui (candlenut)
Name:	The name *Hawaii* probably came from the Polynesian word *Hawaiki*, meaning "homeland"
Motto:	*Ua mau ke ea o ka aina i ka pono* ("The life of the land is perpetuated by righteousness")
Song:	"Hawaii Ponoi" ("Hawaii's Own"). Words by Kalakaua; music by Henry Berger
State capital:	Honolulu, on the island of Oahu
Population:	1,171,592 (1993); ranked 40th
Total area:	6,423 square miles; ranked 47th
Abbreviation:	HI (postal)

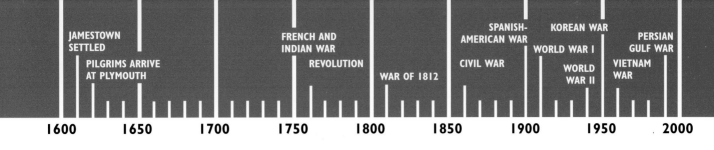

JAMESTOWN SETTLED		FRENCH AND INDIAN WAR			SPANISH-AMERICAN WAR	KOREAN WAR	PERSIAN GULF WAR
PILGRIMS ARRIVE AT PLYMOUTH		REVOLUTION				WORLD WAR I	
			WAR OF 1812		CIVIL WAR	WORLD WAR II	VIETNAM WAR

| 1600 | 1650 | 1700 | 1750 | 1800 | 1850 | 1900 | 1950 | 2000 |

Hawaii is the only state that is made up of islands. It is also the only state located almost entirely in the tropics. Besides its moist, warm climate, it has coral reefs, sandy beaches, and lush mountain scenery. Hawaii is the only state that is not part of the North American continent. Its capital, Honolulu, is about 2,400 miles west of the U.S. mainland. Hawaii is the only state that was once an independent kingdom.

Hawaii consists of a chain of 132 islands in the Pacific. The islands are actually the peaks of huge underwater volcanoes that began erupting millions of years ago. The eight main islands are at the south-eastern end of the chain. Of these, Hawaii is the largest island. Almost 80 percent of the people live on Oahu, the third-largest island.

Tourism is Hawaii's most important industry. Food processing is its main manufacturing activity. Hawaii's tropical climate makes it one of the world's leading producers of pineapples and sugarcane.

IMPORTANT DATES

- **1778:** English explorer Captain James Cook is the first European to visit the Hawaiian islands.
- **1795:** King Kamehameha I unites the Hawaiian islands.
- **1820:** The first missionaries arrive from New England and organize schools.
- **1893:** A revolution overthrows the Hawaiian monarchy.
- **1898:** The United States annexes Hawaii.
- **1903:** An undersea telegraph cable links Hawaii and the mainland United States.
- **1941:** On December 7, the Japanese attack Pearl Harbor, bringing the United States into World War II.
- **1959:** On August 21, Hawaii becomes the 50th state.
- **1980:** The Hawaiian population tops 1 million for the first time.

OF SPECIAL INTEREST

- Polynesians were the first people to live on the Hawaiian islands, first inhabiting them more than 1,000 years ago.
- The Hawaiian alphabet has only 12 letters— a, e, h, i, k, l, m, n, o, p, u, and w.
- Mount Waialeale, on Kauai, is the wettest place on Earth. The average annual rainfall there is 486 inches per year.
- Hawaii is made up of 132 islands. They extend for a distance about equal to that from New York City to Denver, Colorado.
- Mauna Loa, on the island of Hawaii, is the largest active volcano in the world.

Top: A lush Hawaiian rainforest on Oahu.
Bottom: Hibiscus in bloom on Maui.

IDAHO

GEM STATE

Rugged terrain of the
Twin Falls.

State bird: Mountain bluebird
State flower: Syringa (mock orange)
State tree: Western white pine
Name: The name *Idaho* was first proposed
for Colorado but was rejected
because it was not a Native-
American word. It became popular
and was chosen for Idaho in 1863
Motto: *Esto perpetua* ("It is forever")
Song: "Here We Have Idaho." Words
by McKinley Helm and Albert J.
Tompkins; music by
Sallie Hume-Douglas

State capital: Boise
Population: 1,099,096 (1993); ranked 42nd
Total area: 83,574 square miles; ranked 14th
Abbreviation: Ida. (traditional); ID (postal)

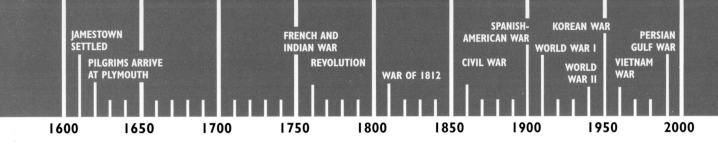

JAMESTOWN SETTLED

PILGRIMS ARRIVE AT PLYMOUTH

FRENCH AND INDIAN WAR

REVOLUTION

WAR OF 1812

SPANISH-AMERICAN WAR

CIVIL WAR

KOREAN WAR

WORLD WAR I

WORLD WAR II

PERSIAN GULF WAR

VIETNAM WAR

1600   1650   1700   1750   1800   1850   1900   1950   2000

Idaho is one of the most scenic states. Idaho's huge, snow-capped mountains are broken by steep canyons. Swirling whitewater rapids contrast with calm, peaceful lakes. Tourists may visit Craters of the Moon National Monument to see the remains of extinct volcanoes or look down on Hells Canyon, the deepest canyon in North America. Coeur d'Alene Lake in the north is thought to be one of the world's most beautiful lakes.

Most of Idaho lies in the rugged Rocky Mountains. In the central and southern parts of the state, the mountains are broken by fertile plains, plateaus, and valleys. Central Idaho contains more than 3 million acres of wilderness, where only pack-horses and mules can navigate the rugged terrain.

Idaho farmers grow sugar beets, wheat, barley, and many other crops, but Idaho is probably most famous for its potatoes. With about 40 percent of the state covered by forest, forest products are one of Idaho's most important industries. Idaho ranks first among the states in silver production.

IMPORTANT DATES

• **1805:** Explorers Meriwether Lewis and William Clark pass through Idaho on their way to the Pacific Ocean.
• **1809:** David Thompson builds the first fur-trading post near Hope and maps the region.
• **1860:** Franklin becomes the first permanent settlement.
• **1879:** Fighting with the Nez Percé and other Native-American peoples ends.
• **1890:** On July 3, Idaho becomes the 43rd state.
• **1965:** Nez Percé National Historical Park is established.

OF SPECIAL INTEREST

• Idaho grows about 12 billion pounds of potatoes each year, more than any other state.
• The Big Wood River is known as the upside-down river. One part flows through a gorge about 100 feet deep and 4 feet wide. Nearby, another part is about 100 feet wide and 4 feet deep.
• In 1951, nuclear energy was first used to generate electricity, near Idaho Falls.

Top: State Capitol, in Boise.
Bottom: Grain elevators in Ashton.

29

ILLINOIS

ILLINOIS

THE PRAIRIE STATE

Sears Tower, the world's tallest building, dominates the Chicago skyline.

State bird:	Cardinal
State flower:	Native violet
State tree:	White oak
Name:	French settlers named the region for the Illinois, or Illini, people. *Illini* is an Algonquin word meaning "men" or "warriors"
Motto:	"State sovereignty, national union"
Song:	"Illinois." Words by Charles H. Chamberlin; music by Archibald Johnston
State capital:	Springfield
Population:	11,697,336 (1993); ranked 6th
Total area:	57,918 square miles; ranked 25th
Abbreviation:	Ill. (traditional); IL (postal)

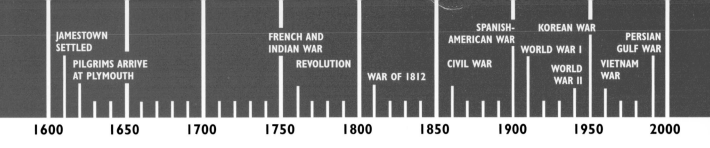

JAMESTOWN SETTLED			FRENCH AND INDIAN WAR			SPANISH-AMERICAN WAR	KOREAN WAR	PERSIAN GULF WAR
PILGRIMS ARRIVE AT PLYMOUTH			REVOLUTION			WORLD WAR I	VIETNAM WAR	
				WAR OF 1812	CIVIL WAR	WORLD WAR II		

1600   1650   1700   1750   1800   1850   1900   1950   2000

Autumn in Matthiessen State Park.

In the heart of the United States, Illinois has the largest population of any midwestern state. It is often called the Land of Lincoln, because Abraham Lincoln lived most of his life there and was buried in Springfield. But Illinois is also sometimes called the Prairie State, because of its rolling, fertile plains. The great Mississippi River forms the western border of Illinois; Lake Michigan forms the northeastern border and provides 63 miles of shoreline and sandy beaches.

Illinois's fertile plains make it an important agricultural state. Its major crops include soybeans, corn, wheat, oats, and sorghum. Still, most people in Illinois live in cities. Chicago, on the shores of Lake Michigan, is the transportation and industrial center of the nation.

Illinois is a leading producer of chemicals, electronics, diesel engines, and earth-moving equipment. The state is also a center for atomic research. Scientists come from all over the world to conduct their research at the Fermi National Accelerator Laboratory near Chicago. The lab has one of the largest atom smashers in the world.

IMPORTANT DATES

• **1673:** French explorers Jacques Marquette and Louis Jolliet enter the Illinois region.
• **1699:** French build a settlement at Cahokia, the oldest town in Illinois.
• **1763:** France cedes the Illinois region to the British after the French and Indian War.
• **1783:** The Illinois region becomes part of the United States at the end of the Revolution.
• **1818:** On December 3, Illinois becomes the 21st state.
• **1871:** A fire destroys most of Chicago.
• **1973:** Sears Tower, the world's tallest building, is completed in Chicago.

OF SPECIAL INTEREST

• Springfield became the state capital in 1837, thanks largely to the efforts of Abraham Lincoln, then a 28-year-old state assemblyman.
• The first successful railroad sleeping car was built by George Pullman in Bloomington in 1858.
• The first metal skyscraper was built in Chicago in 1884 and 1885. It was ten stories high.
• The first controlled nuclear chain reaction occurred at the University of Chicago in 1942.

Fermi National Accelerator Laboratory, in Batavia.

31

INDIANA

HOOSIER STATE

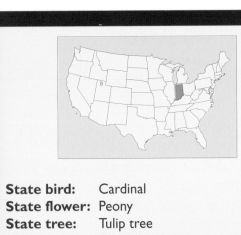

Bathers enjoy Dunes State Park, on Lake Michigan.

State bird: Cardinal
State flower: Peony
State tree: Tulip tree
Name: The name *Indiana* comes from the word *Indian*
Motto: "The crossroads of America"
Song: "On the Banks of the Wabash, Far Away." Words and music by Paul Dresser
State capital: Indianapolis
Population: 5,712,799 (1993); ranked 14th
Total area: 36,420 square miles; ranked 38th
Abbreviation: Ind. (traditional); IN (postal)

JAMESTOWN SETTLED		FRENCH AND INDIAN WAR			SPANISH-AMERICAN WAR	KOREAN WAR	PERSIAN GULF WAR
PILGRIMS ARRIVE AT PLYMOUTH		REVOLUTION				WORLD WAR I	
			WAR OF 1812		CIVIL WAR	WORLD WAR II / VIETNAM WAR	

| 1600 | 1650 | 1700 | 1750 | 1800 | 1850 | 1900 | 1950 | 2000 |

Indiana is a state of many landscapes. Lakes and streams provide opportunities for boating, fishing, and swimming. Each year, thousands of people visit the famous Indiana Dunes National Lakeshore, along Lake Michigan. Artists and nature lovers are also attracted to the colorful, rolling hills of south-central Indiana.

Broad, fertile plains cover more than half of Indiana, making it one of the top ten farm states. These plains are part of what is commonly called the Midwestern Corn Belt. The northwestern corner of Indiana borders on Lake Michigan. The state's southern border is formed by the Ohio River, which is surrounded by forested hills.

Indiana's most important crop is corn. Other major farm products are wheat, soybeans, cattle, hogs, milk, and eggs. Indiana is also a great steel-producing center. Its other industries include electrical machinery, food products, transportation equipment, and chemicals.

Autumn on a university campus.

IMPORTANT DATES

• **1679:** Sieur de La Salle becomes the first European to explore the Indiana region.
• **c. 1731:** The French found Indiana's first permanent European settlement at Vincennes.
• **1783:** The British cede the Indiana region to the United States.
• **1816:** On December 11, Indiana becomes the 19th state.
• **c. 1906:** The city of Gary is founded for steel workers.
• **1949:** Indiana schools are racially integrated by an act of the state legislature.
• **1981:** Indiana settles a long-running border dispute with Kentucky and Ohio.

OF SPECIAL INTEREST

• The Raggedy Ann Doll was created in Indianapolis in 1914.
• The first professional baseball game was played in Fort Wayne on May 4, 1871.
• Indiana has the only town with the name Santa Claus. It receives more than half a million pieces of Christmas mail each year.

Top left: An old-fashioned outdoor barbecue.
Bottom left: The Ohio River.

IOWA

HAWKEYE STATE

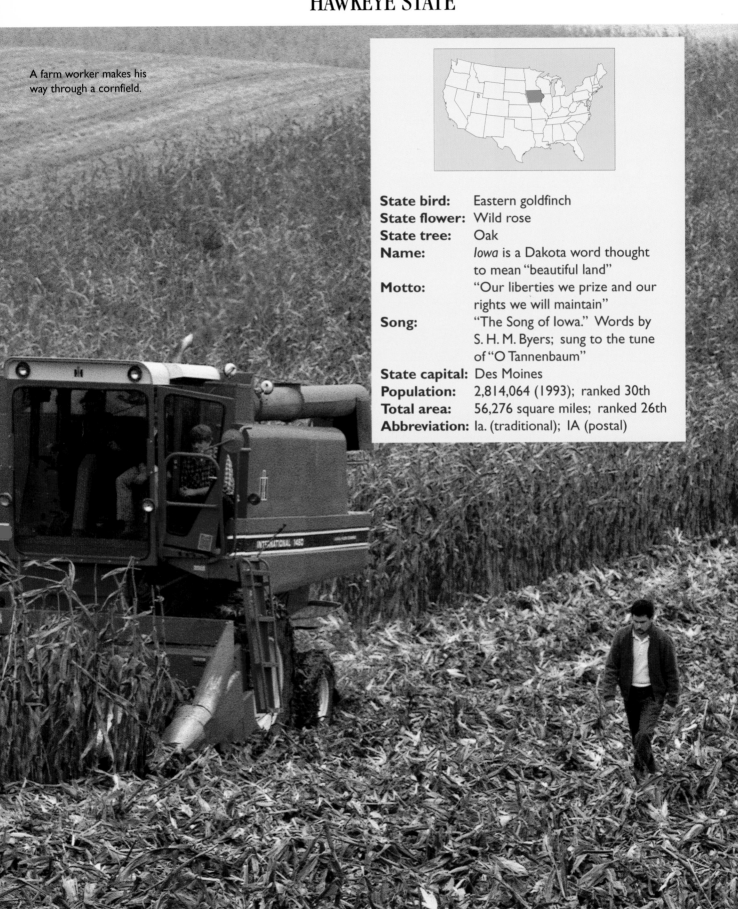

A farm worker makes his way through a cornfield.

State bird: Eastern goldfinch
State flower: Wild rose
State tree: Oak
Name: *Iowa* is a Dakota word thought to mean "beautiful land"
Motto: "Our liberties we prize and our rights we will maintain"
Song: "The Song of Iowa." Words by S. H. M. Byers; sung to the tune of "O Tannenbaum"
State capital: Des Moines
Population: 2,814,064 (1993); ranked 30th
Total area: 56,276 square miles; ranked 26th
Abbreviation: Ia. (traditional); IA (postal)

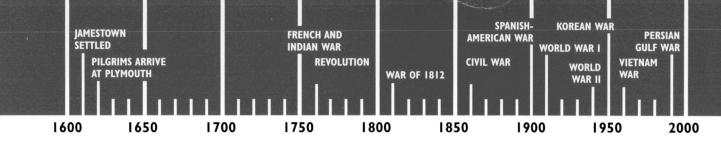

JAMESTOWN
SETTLED

PILGRIMS ARRIVE
AT PLYMOUTH

FRENCH AND
INDIAN WAR

REVOLUTION

WAR OF 1812

SPANISH-
AMERICAN WAR

CIVIL WAR

KOREAN WAR

WORLD WAR I

WORLD
WAR II

PERSIAN
GULF WAR

VIETNAM
WAR

1600   1650   1700   1750   1800   1850   1900   1950   2000

During the last Ice Age, glaciers moved over what is now Iowa, cutting off hill tops and filling in valleys. As a result, most of Iowa is gently rolling plains. The Mississippi River forms Iowa's eastern border. The Big

Sioux and Missouri Rivers form its western border. The rivers provide irrigation water in times of drought and serve as waterways for shipping.

Iowa has about a third of the best farmland in the United States. In one way or another, most Iowans depend on their state's rich soil and the crops it produces. Iowa's farms provide about seven percent of the nation's food supply. The chief crops are corn and soybeans. More hogs are raised in Iowa than in any other state.

Among Iowa's leading industries are the production of farm machinery and food processing. Sioux City has the nation's largest popcorn-processing plant, and Cedar Rapids has one of the largest cereal mills.

IMPORTANT DATES

• **1673:** French explorers Jacques Marquette and Louis Joliet are the first white people to explore parts of Iowa.
• **1788:** Julian Dubuque of France becomes Iowa's first white settler.
• **1803:** The United States acquires Iowa from France in the Louisiana Purchase.
• **1832:** Black Hawk, leader of the Sauk and Fox tribes, is defeated in a war against white settlers.
• **1846:** On December 28, Iowa becomes the 29th state.
• **1856:** The first bridge across the Mississippi River is built at Davenport.
• **1993:** Heavy rains cause the Mississippi and other rivers to swell, creating the worst floods of the century.

OF SPECIAL INTEREST

• The shortest and steepest U.S. railroad is in Dubuque. It is 296 feet long and rises at a 60-degree incline to a height of 189 feet.
• The top-selling apple in the United States, the Red Delicious, was developed at an orchard near East Peru.
• Iowa grows more corn than any other state— about 1.4 billion bushels a year.
• Ancient Native-American burial mounds at Effigy National Monument were built in the shapes of birds and bears. The mounds were constructed by the Hopewellian culture about 2,500 years ago.

Top: State Capitol, in Des Moines.
Bottom: A scenic rural village called St. Donatus.

35

KANSAS

SUNFLOWER STATE

A wheat field is harvested during sunset in western Kansas.

State bird: Western meadowlark
State flower: Sunflower
State tree: Cottonwood
Name: Kansas was named for the Kansa tribe of Native Americans. *Kansa* means "wind people"
Motto: *Ad astra per aspera* ("To the stars through difficulties")
Song: "Home on the Range." Words by Brewster Higley; music by Daniel Kelly
State capital: Topeka
Population: 2,530,746 (1993); ranked 32nd
Total area: 82,282 square miles; ranked 14th
Abbreviation: Kan. (traditional); KS (postal)

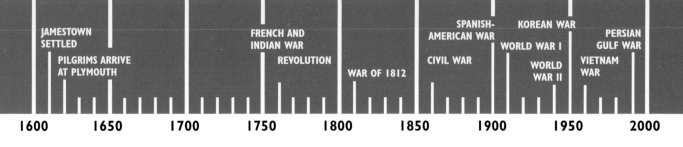

JAMESTOWN
SETTLED

PILGRIMS ARRIVE
AT PLYMOUTH

FRENCH AND
INDIAN WAR
REVOLUTION

WAR OF 1812

SPANISH-
AMERICAN WAR

CIVIL WAR

KOREAN WAR

WORLD WAR I

WORLD
WAR II

PERSIAN
GULF WAR

VIETNAM
WAR

1600   1650   1700   1750   1800   1850   1900   1950   2000

Kansas was once at the heart of the western frontier. Thousands of wagon trains rolled through the state, carrying settlers to California. After the railroad reached the state in the 1860s, Texas cowboys drove their herds to Kansas for shipment east. Wild cow towns sprang up. Today, some of the Wild West is preserved at Dodge City. There, one can see many restored saloons, stores, wagons, and stagecoaches from America's frontier past.

Flat or gently rolling plains cover most of Kansas. Winds move easily across the plains, so the weather in the state changes quickly. Kansas has cold winters and warm summers. Tornadoes, hail, blizzards, and thunderstorms are all part of typical Kansas weather.

Kansas grows more wheat than any other state. About 400 million bushels of wheat are normally produced each year. Kansas mills grind the wheat into flour and ship it around the world. In addition, Kansas ranks among the leading states in the

production of beef cattle. About 65,000 oil and gas wells dot the Kansas prairie. The state is also one of the largest producers of airplanes.

IMPORTANT DATES
- **1541:** Spanish explorer Francisco Vásquez de Coronado reaches central Kansas.
- **1803:** The United States purchases most of Kansas from France in the Louisiana Purchase.
- **1861:** On January 29, Kansas becomes the 34th state.
- **1894:** Kansas oil and gas fields begin production.
- **1934-1935:** Huge dust storms damage large areas of Kansas farmland.
- **1976:** The Mid-American All-Indian Center opens near Kansas City.
- **1988:** Severe drought damages more than 865,000 acres of farmland.

OF SPECIAL INTEREST
- Lebanon, in north-central Kansas, is located at the geographic center of the 48 contiguous United States.
- When the Territory of Kansas was formed in 1854, it became a battleground between supporters and opponents of slavery.
- In the 1800s, pioneers passed through Kansas on the Oregon and Santa Fe Trails. Abilene marked the end of the Chisolm Trail, over which Texas cattle were driven to market.
- Susanna Salter was elected the first woman mayor in the United States. She was elected the mayor of Argonia in 1887.

Top: Performers walk the streets of historic Front Street in Dodge City.
Bottom: State Capitol, in Topeka.

37

KENTUCKY

BLUEGRASS STATE

Horses graze on bluegrass on one of Kentucky's many horse farms.

State bird: Kentucky cardinal
State flower: Goldenrod
State tree: Kentucky coffeetree
Name: Kentucky gets its name from the Wyandot word *Kentake*, meaning "meadowland" or "prairie"
Motto: "United we stand, divided we fall"
Song: "My Old Kentucky Home." Words and music by Stephen Foster
State capital: Frankfort
Population: 3,788,808 (1993); ranked 24th
Total area: 40,411 square miles; ranked 37th
Abbreviation: Ken. (traditional); KY (postal)

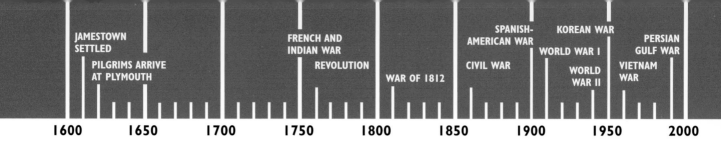

JAMESTOWN SETTLED		FRENCH AND INDIAN WAR			SPANISH-AMERICAN WAR	KOREAN WAR	PERSIAN GULF WAR
PILGRIMS ARRIVE AT PLYMOUTH		REVOLUTION		CIVIL WAR	WORLD WAR I	VIETNAM WAR	
			WAR OF 1812		WORLD WAR II		

1600   1650   1700   1750   1800   1850   1900   1950   2000

Rivers have been important to Kentucky since early times. The Ohio River, which forms the state's northern border, carried explorers into the region. As settlements grew, boats carried supplies and farm products along this river and the many others that feed into it. Kentucky's rivers are still important for transportation. A number have been dammed, to create reservoirs, control floods, and provide hydroelectric power.

The Appalachian Mountains cut across the eastern part of Kentucky. This region consists of

beautiful forested mountains, valleys, rivers, and streams. The north-central part of the state is made up of rolling fields where horses and cattle graze. The state takes its nickname from the bluegrass pastures in this region.

Kentucky is largely a rural state. Farming is an important industry, with tobacco, soybeans, and wheat among the leading crops. The state ranks first in the breeding of thoroughbred racehorses. It also leads the nation in the manufacture of bourbon whiskey and is a major coal producer.

IMPORTANT DATES
• **1750:** Pioneer scout Thomas Walker explores what is now Kentucky.
• **1774:** Harrodstown (now Harrodsburg) becomes the first permanent Kentucky settlement.
• **1792:** On June 1, Kentucky becomes the 15th state.
• **1875:** The first Kentucky Derby horse race is run at Churchill Downs, in Louisville.
• **1966:** Kentucky is the first southern state to pass a comprehensive civil rights law.

OF SPECIAL INTEREST
• Native Americans may have first lived in western Kentucky as long as 10,000 years ago.
• Daniel Boone explored Kentucky from 1769 to 1771. In 1775, he blazed a trail through the Cumberland Gap to the site of Boonesboro.
• The world's first free-flowing oil well was drilled near Burkesville, in 1829.
• The Mammoth-Fling cave system is the largest known cave system in the world. It is entirely located within the state of Kentucky.
• The U.S. government gold depository at Fort Knox contains more than $6 billion in gold bullion.

Top: Abraham Lincoln's boyhood home at Knob Creek.
Bottom: Drying Kentucky tobacco.

LOUISIANA

PELICAN STATE

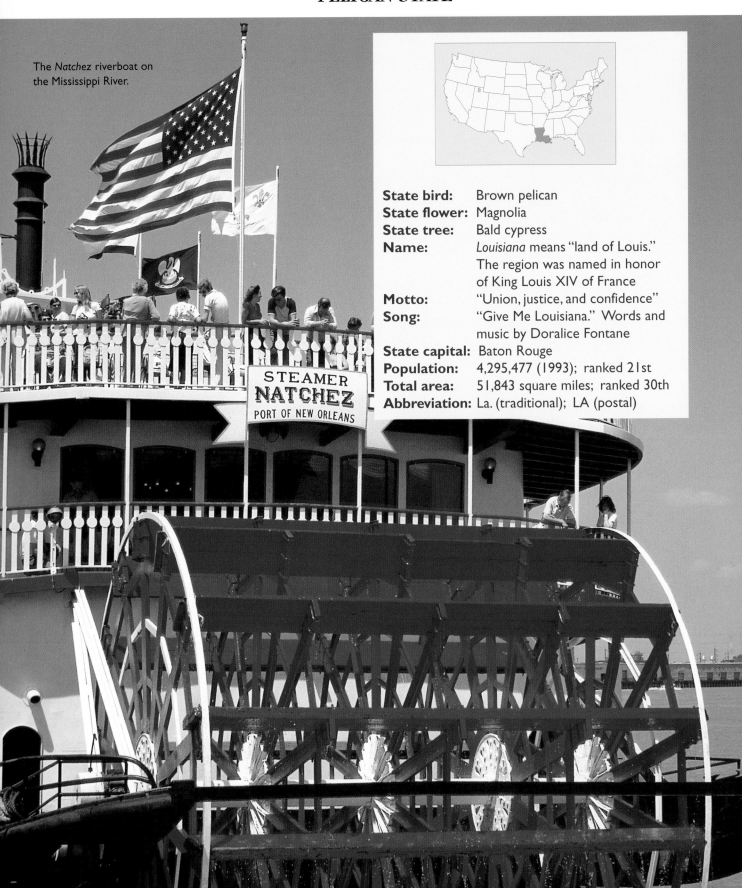

The *Natchez* riverboat on the Mississippi River.

STEAMER NATCHEZ
PORT OF NEW ORLEANS

State bird:	Brown pelican
State flower:	Magnolia
State tree:	Bald cypress
Name:	*Louisiana* means "land of Louis." The region was named in honor of King Louis XIV of France
Motto:	"Union, justice, and confidence"
Song:	"Give Me Louisiana." Words and music by Doralice Fontane
State capital:	Baton Rouge
Population:	4,295,477 (1993); ranked 21st
Total area:	51,843 square miles; ranked 30th
Abbreviation:	La. (traditional); LA (postal)

JAMESTOWN SETTLED		FRENCH AND INDIAN WAR			SPANISH-AMERICAN WAR	KOREAN WAR		PERSIAN GULF WAR
PILGRIMS ARRIVE AT PLYMOUTH			REVOLUTION		WORLD WAR I		
				WAR OF 1812	CIVIL WAR	WORLD WAR II	VIETNAM WAR

| 1600 | 1650 | 1700 | 1750 | 1800 | 1850 | 1900 | 1950 | 2000 |

Louisiana has a rich blend of cultures. Spanish and French influences can still be seen in buildings from colonial times. The Louisiana Cajuns are descendants of French-speaking people who arrived in the region from Acadia, in Canada, in the 1700s. They are famous for their spicy cooking and lively music. Even more famous is New Orleans jazz, just one of the many contributions of Louisiana's African Americans. All these cultures come together during Louisiana's best-known event: Mardi Gras, the huge, riotous carnival held each year in New Orleans.

Louisiana has been important throughout U.S. history because it lies at the mouth of the Mississippi River, the main water route to the American heartland. Along the coast of the Gulf of Mexico, much of the land is below sea level and must be protected by dikes and levees. Bayous—swampy streams—lead through cypress swamps. Away from the coast are fertile farmlands and rolling hills covered with pine forests.

Louisiana is a major producer of petroleum and natural gas. In addition, it is the leading salt-producing state. Among its chief crops are soybeans, sugarcane, rice, sweet potatoes, and pecans. Louisiana also supplies about one quarter of all the fish caught in the United States.

IMPORTANT DATES

• **1541:** Spanish explorer Hernando de Soto explores northern Louisiana.
• **1682:** French explorer Sieur de La Salle reaches the mouth of the Mississippi and claims the region for France.
• **1714:** Natchitoches becomes the first permanent town in Louisiana.
• **1803:** The United States acquires Louisiana from France in the Louisiana Purchase.
• **1812:** On April 30, Louisiana becomes the 18th state.
• **1838:** The first Mardi Gras parade is held in New Orleans.
• **1879:** The mouth of the Mississippi River is deepened to allow large oceangoing ships to reach New Orleans.
• **1927:** The Mississippi River floods, causing immense damage.
• **1992:** Hurricane Andrew crashes into the Louisiana coast.

OF SPECIAL INTEREST

• The St. Louis Cathedral in New Orleans is the oldest cathedral in continual use in the United States. It was built in 1716.
• Avery Island, near Iberia, has the oldest salt mine in the Western Hemisphere.
• Louisiana has three of the largest egret colonies in the country.
• More catfish are raised in Louisiana than in any other place in the world.
• The Port of New Orleans handles more shipping than any other port in the United States.

Top: A brown pelican, the state bird.
Bottom: A terrace in the French Quarter of New Orleans.

41

MAINE

PINE TREE STATE

The Portland Headlight, one of Maine's many lighthouses.

State bird:	Chickadee
State flower:	White pine cone and tassel
State tree:	White pine
Name:	*Maine* probably means "mainland." It may have been named by the French, after a region in France
Motto:	*Dirigo* ("I direct")
Song:	"State of Maine Song." Words and music by Roger Vinton Snow
State capital:	Augusta
Population:	1,239,448 (1993); ranked 39th
Total area:	35,387 square miles; ranked 39th
Abbreviation:	Me. (traditional); ME (postal)

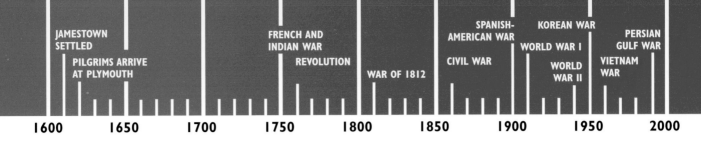

JAMESTOWN SETTLED		FRENCH AND INDIAN WAR			SPANISH-AMERICAN WAR	KOREAN WAR	PERSIAN GULF WAR
PILGRIMS ARRIVE AT PLYMOUTH		REVOLUTION			WORLD WAR I	VIETNAM WAR
			WAR OF 1812	CIVIL WAR	WORLD WAR II
1600	1650	1700	1750	1800	1850	1900	1950	2000

Maine is best known for the rugged beauty of its Atlantic coastline. Jagged rocks and steep cliffs alternate with sandy beaches and quiet coves. Lighthouses, vacation resorts, and fishing villages line the coast. There are also thousands of offshore islands, bays, and inlets to explore.

Away from the coast, the land rises in rolling hills and low mountains. Pine forests cover the mountains, and there are thousands of sparkling lakes and quick-flowing streams and rivers. Maine's wilderness areas provide opportunities for boating, skiing, fishing, hunting, and other outdoor activities.

The forests provide the material for Maine's important wood-processing industry. Factories turn wood into paper, pulp, toothpicks, and many more products. Other industries manufacture electronic

equipment, footwear, textiles, machinery, and ships. Maine is also a farming state. Major crops include potatoes, oats, apples, and blueberries. And with its long coastline, Maine is an important fishing state. More lobsters are trapped off the Maine coast than anyplace else in the United States.

IMPORTANT DATES

• **1497-1499:** Explorers John and Sebastian Cabot sail along the coast of Maine.
• **1607:** English settlers establish the Popham Colony, near the mouth of the Kennebec River. They leave a year later.
• **1616:** A permanent settlement is founded near Biddeford.
• **1691:** Maine becomes part of Massachusetts.
• **1820:** On March 15, Maine becomes the 23rd state.
• **1842:** A long-running dispute over the Maine-Canada border is settled by treaty.
• **1976:** A 40,000-acre wilderness preserve is approved on Bigelow Mountain.
• **1980:** The U.S. government pays $81.5 million to Native Americans of Maine for lands taken from their ancestors during the 1700s and 1800s.

OF SPECIAL INTEREST

• Vikings from Scandinavia probably visited the Maine coast almost 1,000 years ago.
• Chester Greenwood of Farmington patented the first earmuffs on March 13, 1877.
• The Camp Fire Girls originated at Sebago Lake in 1910.
• The Portland Headlight at Portland is the oldest lighthouse in use in the United States. It began service in 1791.
• West Quoddy Head is the most easterly point of land in the continental United States.
• Maine produces more wooden toothpicks than any other state.

Top: A traditional Maine lobster bake.
Bottom: State Capitol, in Augusta.

43

MARYLAND

OLD LINE STATE; FREE STATE

A road winds through Baltimore County's picturesque Worthington Valley.

State bird: Baltimore oriole
State flower: Black-eyed susan
State tree: White oak
Name: Maryland was named for queen Henrietta Maria of England
Motto: *Fatti maschii, parole femine* ("Manly deeds, womanly words")
Song: "Maryland! My Maryland!" Words by James Ryder Randall, sung to the tune of "O Tannenbaum"
State capital: Annapolis
Population: 4,964,898 (1993); ranked 19th
Total area: 12,407 square miles; ranked 42nd
Abbreviation: Md. (traditional); MD (postal)

JAMESTOWN SETTLED		FRENCH AND INDIAN WAR				SPANISH-AMERICAN WAR	KOREAN WAR		PERSIAN GULF WAR
PILGRIMS ARRIVE AT PLYMOUTH		REVOLUTION				CIVIL WAR	WORLD WAR I	VIETNAM WAR	
				WAR OF 1812			WORLD WAR II		

| 1600 | 1650 | 1700 | 1750 | 1800 | 1850 | 1900 | 1950 | 2000 |

The Chesapeake Bay cuts deep into eastern Maryland. Its many fine harbors made Maryland a center of trade during colonial times. Shipping is still important, and so is fishing. Maryland is famous for its clams, oysters, and crabs. And the bay's long shoreline provides residents and visitors alike with places for swimming and boating.

Chesapeake Bay divides Maryland into two parts. The land east of the bay is called the Eastern Shore. Southern Maryland, south of Washington, D.C., is mostly low and flat. Western Maryland is a region of mountains, river valleys, and rolling hills.

Tobacco is an important crop in southern Maryland. Other Maryland farms raise poultry and dairy cattle and grow corn, soybeans, vegetables, and grains. Apples are grown in the western part of the state. Major industries include the manufacture of electronic equipment, production of chemicals, and food processing. A large number of Maryland's people work for government, many for the federal government in Washington, D.C.

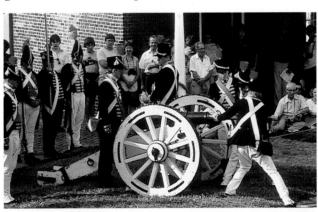

IMPORTANT DATES

- **1608:** Captain John Smith of England explores the Chesapeake Bay region.
- **1632:** England's King Charles I grants the province of Maryland to Cecil Calvert, the second Lord Baltimore.
- **1784:** The Continental Congress meets at Annapolis to approve the treaty ending the Revolutionary War.
- **1788:** On April 28, Maryland becomes the 7th state.
- **1791:** Maryland gives land for the District of Columbia (Washington, D.C.).
- **1828:** Construction begins on the Baltimore & Ohio Railroad, the first passenger railroad in the United States.
- **1864:** During the Civil War, Confederate forces invade Maryland but are driven out. Maryland adopts a state constitution abolishing slavery.
- **1983:** The state begins a program to improve water quality in Chesapeake Bay.

OF SPECIAL INTEREST

- Francis Scott Key wrote the "Star-Spangled Banner" after watching the British attack on Fort McHenry, near Baltimore, during the War of 1812.
- The first U.S. telegraph line connected Baltimore to Washington, D.C., in 1844.
- The first elevated electric railroad in the country was built in 1893 in Baltimore.
- Jousting is the official state sport of Maryland. "Knights" on horseback gallop at full speed, trying to spear a ring with their lances.

Top: The National Aquarium, at Baltimore's Inner Harbor.
Bottom: A re-enactment at Fort McHenry.

MASSACHUSETTS

BAY STATE; OLD COLONY

A farm worker stands in a wet bog of cranberries.

State bird: Chickadee
State flower: Mayflower (trailing arbutus)
State tree: American elm
Name: Massachusetts was named after the Massachuset tribe, which lived near present-day Boston
Motto: *Ense petit placidam sub libertate quietem* ("By the sword we seek peace, but peace only under liberty")
Song: "All Hail to Massachusetts." Words and music by Arthur J. Marsh
State capital: Boston
Population: 6,012,268 (1993); ranked 13th
Total area: 10,555 square miles; ranked 43rd
Abbreviation: Mass. (traditional); MA (postal)

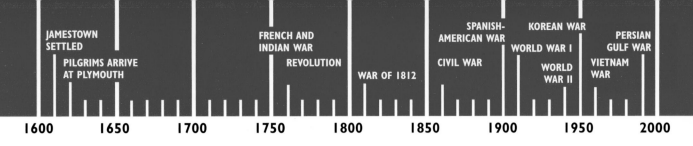

JAMESTOWN SETTLED		FRENCH AND INDIAN WAR			SPANISH-AMERICAN WAR	KOREAN WAR	PERSIAN GULF WAR	
PILGRIMS ARRIVE AT PLYMOUTH		REVOLUTION				WORLD WAR I		
			WAR OF 1812	CIVIL WAR		WORLD WAR II	VIETNAM WAR	

| 1600 | 1650 | 1700 | 1750 | 1800 | 1850 | 1900 | 1950 | 2000 |

Massachusetts is a state steeped in history. In 1620, the Pilgrims settled Plymouth, the second permanent English settlement (after Jamestown, Virginia) in what became the United States. It was in Massachusetts that the Revolutionary War began. The pride that Massachusetts takes in its history is reflected in the many historical sites preserved around the state.

The Massachusetts landscape is covered with hills and valleys. The Atlantic Ocean is on its eastern border, making such cities and towns as Boston,

Gloucester, and New Bedford important ports. Cape Cod is a famous summer resort. At the center of the state, rich farmland lies all along the Connecticut River. West of the river, and bordering New York State, are the Berkshire Hills.

The major industries of Massachusetts include the manufacture of electronic equipment, books, and textiles. Massachusetts farms produce cranberries, many kinds of vegetables, and dairy products. The state also has a large fishing industry. Greater Boston is a business and cultural center. It is known for its colleges and universities, which include Harvard University and the Massachusetts Institute of Technology (M.I.T.).

IMPORTANT DATES

- **1620:** Pilgrims land and found Plymouth.
- **1630:** Puritans found Boston.
- **1773:** The Boston Tea Party takes place: Patriots dump tea into Boston Harbor to protest a tea tax.
- **1775:** The Revolutionary War begins at Lexington and Concord.
- **1788:** On February 6, Massachusetts becomes the 6th state.
- **1960:** John F. Kennedy, born in Brookline, is elected the 35th president of the United States.

OF SPECIAL INTEREST

- The first post office in the United States was established in Boston in 1639.
- The telephone was invented by Alexander Graham Bell in Boston and patented in 1876.
- Basketball was invented by James Naismith in Springfield in 1891.
- Boston opened the first subway in the country in 1897.
- The first baseball World Series was played in Boston from October 1 to October 13, 1903.

Top: The Boston skyline.
Bottom: A scenic beach on Cape Cod.

MICHIGAN

GREAT LAKES STATE; WOLVERINE STATE

State bird:	Robin
State flower:	Apple blossom
State tree:	White pine
Name:	Michigan is named for Lake Michigan. The Ojibwa people called the lake *Michigama*, which means "great lake"
Motto:	*Si quaeris peninsulam amoenam, circumspice* ("If you seek a pleasant peninsula, look about you")
Song:	"Michigan, My Michigan." Words by Giles Kavanagh; music by H. J. O'Reilly Clint
State capital:	Lansing
Population:	9,477,545 (1994); ranked 8th
Total area:	96,705 square miles; ranked 11th
Abbreviation:	Mich. (traditional); MI (postal)

Apple blossoms in bloom at Benton Harbor.

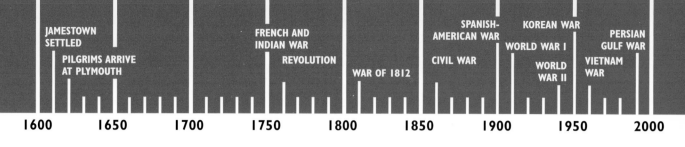

JAMESTOWN SETTLED

PILGRIMS ARRIVE AT PLYMOUTH

FRENCH AND INDIAN WAR

REVOLUTION

WAR OF 1812

SPANISH-AMERICAN WAR

CIVIL WAR

KOREAN WAR

WORLD WAR I

WORLD WAR II

VIETNAM WAR

PERSIAN GULF WAR

1600   1650   1700   1750   1800   1850   1900   1950   2000

Michigan is most famous as the center of the American automobile industry. But the state has much to offer—beaches and resorts along the Great Lakes, thousands of smaller inland lakes, and vast areas of forest. These attractions draw more than 22 million visitors to Michigan each year.

Michigan is divided into two parts completely separated by water—the Upper Peninsula and the Lower Peninsula. The Lower Peninsula touches on four of the five Great Lakes, making many of its cities busy ports. The state's shoreline—more than 3,100 miles—is longer than that of any other state except Alaska.

In automobile manufacturing, Michigan leads the nation. Detroit alone produces more cars and trucks than any other state. Michigan is also important in food processing and steel production. Its farms raise cattle and produce dairy products, fruits, and vegetables.

IMPORTANT DATES

• **c. 1620:** The French explorer Étienne Brûlé visits Michigan's Upper Peninsula.
• **1668:** French explorer Father Jacques Marquette founds Sault Ste. Marie, Michigan's first permanent settlement.
• **1783:** Great Britain grants Michigan to the United States.
• **1837:** On January 26, Michigan becomes the 26th state.
• **1899:** Ransom E. Olds establishes Michigan's first automobile factory, in Detroit.
• **1957:** Mackinac Bridge is completed over the Straits of Mackinac, connecting the Upper and Lower Peninsulas.
• **1988:** The Enrico Fermi II nuclear power plant begins operation near Detroit.

OF SPECIAL INTEREST

• The Republican Party formally adopted its name at Jackson in 1854.
• Michigan State University, founded in 1855, is the world's oldest agricultural college.
• The first lines to mark traffic lanes were painted near Trenton in 1911.
• Battle Creek, called the Cereal Bowl of America, produces more breakfast cereal than any other city in the world.
• The Soo Canals at Sault Ste. Marie are among the busiest ship canals in all of the Western Hemisphere.

Top: Soo Canals at Sault Ste. Marie.
Bottom: The Detroit skyline at night.

49

MINNESOTA

NORTH STAR STATE; GOPHER STATE

Pipestone Creek, at
Pipestone National
Monument.

State bird: Common loon
State flower: Pink-and-white lady's slipper
State tree: Norway pine
Name: The name *Minnesota* is from two Sioux words—*minni*, meaning "water," and *sotah*, meaning "sky-tinted" or "clouded"
Motto: *L'étoile du nord* ("The star of the north")
Song: "Hail! Minnesota." Words by Truman E. Rickard and Arthur E. Upson; music by Truman E. Rickard
State capital: St. Paul
Population: 4,517,416 (1990); ranked 20th
Total area: 86,943 square miles; ranked 13th
Abbreviation: Minn. (traditional); MN (postal)

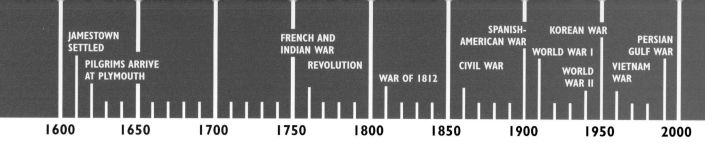

JAMESTOWN SETTLED

PILGRIMS ARRIVE AT PLYMOUTH

FRENCH AND INDIAN WAR

REVOLUTION

WAR OF 1812

SPANISH-AMERICAN WAR

CIVIL WAR

KOREAN WAR

WORLD WAR I

WORLD WAR II

PERSIAN GULF WAR

VIETNAM WAR

1600   1650   1700   1750   1800   1850   1900   1950   2000

Minnesota is sometimes called the Land of 10,000 Lakes. Actually, more than 15,000 lakes are scattered across the state. The many lakes and pine forests contribute to Minnesota's natural beauty.

The northeastern part of Minnesota borders on Lake Superior. Its rocky cliffs and dense forests make it one of Minnesota's most popular vacation areas. Most of the rest of the state is covered by flat or gently rolling plains. Winter winds whipping across the plains bring subzero temperatures from Canada. Summers are short and hot.

Lumber, iron ore, and wheat were once the state's main products. But many forests have been cut down, and iron deposits are running out. And in the 1930s, soil erosion forced farmers to turn to other crops. Minnesota farmers now raise such crops as corn, soybeans, and sugar beets. Minnesota is also an important dairy state. But most of the state's people work in manufacturing and service industries. Minneapolis and St. Paul, called the Twin Cities, are the cultural and industrial heart of Minnesota.

IMPORTANT DATES

• **c. 1660:** French fur traders enter the region that today is Minnesota.

• **1679:** Daniel Greysolon, Sieur Duluth, explores the western shore of Lake Superior.

• **1763:** Great Britain gains eastern Minnesota from France.

• **1783:** Great Britain grants eastern Minnesota to the United States.

• **1803:** The United States acquires western Minnesota from France in the Louisiana Purchase.

• **1858:** On May 11, Minnesota becomes the 32nd state.

• **1865:** Rich iron deposits are discovered.

• **1959:** The St. Lawrence Seaway provides Minnesota with a water route leading to the Atlantic Ocean.

OF SPECIAL INTEREST

• The source of the Mississippi River is located at Lake Itasca, in northwestern Minnesota. It was discovered by explorer Henry Schoolcraft in 1832.

• Transparent cellophane tape was invented in St. Paul by Richard Gurley Drew in 1930.

• The Northwest Angle, an area that juts into Canada at Lake of the Woods, is farther north than any part of the United States except Alaska.

• The Mayo Clinic, in Rochester, is a world-famous medical center.

Top: State Capitol, in St. Paul.
Bottom: Minnesota's state bird, the common loon.

MISSISSIPPI

MAGNOLIA STATE

Longwood, an antebellum home whose construction was halted by the start of the Civil War, in Natchez.

State bird: Mockingbird
State flower: Magnolia
State tree: Magnolia
Name: The name *Mississippi* comes from Native-American words that mean "great water" or "father of water"
Motto: *Virtute et armis* ("By valor and arms")
Song: "Go, Mississippi." Words and music by Houston Davis
State capital: Jackson
Population: 2,642,748 (1993); ranked 31st
Total area: 48,434 square miles; ranked 32nd
Abbreviation: Miss. (traditional); MS (postal)

JAMESTOWN
SETTLED

PILGRIMS ARRIVE
AT PLYMOUTH

FRENCH AND
INDIAN WAR
REVOLUTION

WAR OF 1812

SPANISH-
AMERICAN WAR

CIVIL WAR

KOREAN WAR

WORLD WAR I

WORLD
WAR II

PERSIAN
GULF WAR

VIETNAM
WAR

1600   1650   1700   1750   1800   1850   1900   1950   2000

Mississippi is part of the Deep South. Its people are proud of their state's traditions and history. Reminders of the Old South can be seen in the stately antebellum (pre-Civil War) mansions scattered throughout the state. Many important battles of the Civil War were fought in Mississippi. Today, monuments recall these and other events in the state's history.

Mississippi has 44 miles of coastline along the Gulf of Mexico. The Mississippi River forms the state's western border. The land along the river is low, so dams and levees have been built to control flooding. But floods are still quite common, especially in the delta region, where the river meets the gulf. Most of the rest of the state is farmland and pine-covered hills. Mississippi has warm, moist summers and mild, short winters.

Cotton was Mississippi's main product in its early days. Cotton is still grown, along with soybeans and other crops. Mississippi produces petroleum, lumber, and a variety of other manufactured goods. Shrimp fishing and catfish farming are also important industries.

IMPORTANT DATES

• **1540:** Spanish explorer Hernando de Soto passes through the Mississippi region.
• **1682:** French explorer Sieur de La Salle claims the Mississippi Valley as part of France.
• **1699:** The first permanent white settlement in Mississippi is established at Fort Maurepas.
• **1817:** On December 10, Mississippi becomes the 20th state.
• **1861:** Mississippi joins the Confederacy in the Civil War.
• **1909:** The boll weevil invades the state and severely damages the cotton crop.
• **1969:** Hurricane Camille wreaks havoc along the Gulf Coast.
• **1985:** The Tennessee-Tombigbee Waterway is completed, linking the Tennessee River to the Gulf of Mexico.

OF SPECIAL INTEREST

• The Natchez Trace is an old route from Natchez to Nashville, Tennessee. Today, it includes parks, hiking trails, and historic sites.
• Coca-Cola was first bottled by Joseph A. Biedenharn in Vicksburg in 1894.
• The world's first human heart transplant took place at the University of Mississippi Medical Center in 1964.

Top: State flower, the magnolia.
Bottom: Old cotton looms, in Natchez.

MISSOURI

SHOW ME STATE

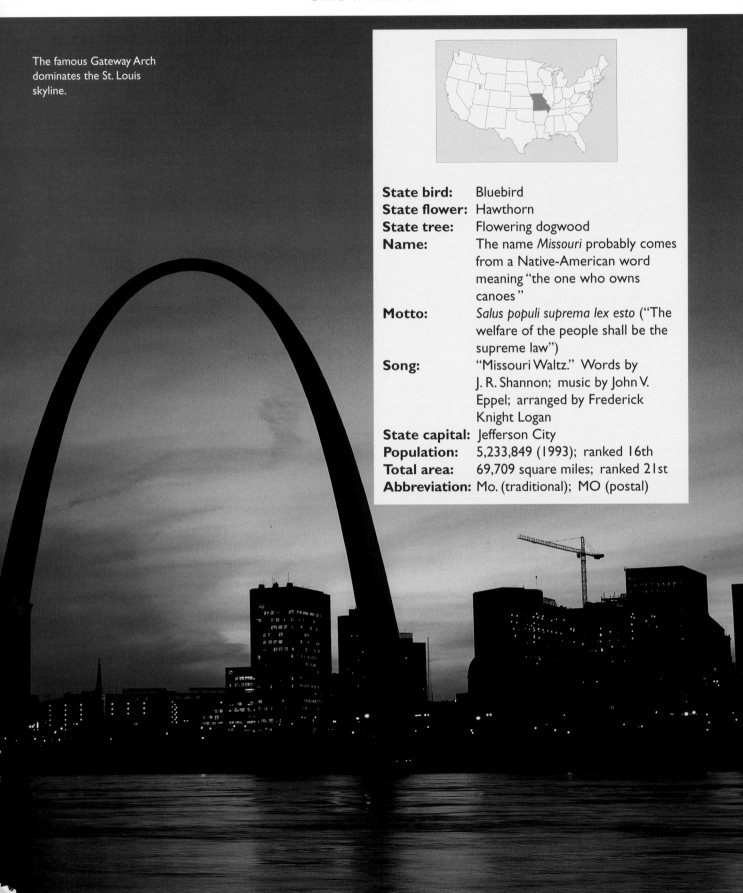

The famous Gateway Arch dominates the St. Louis skyline.

State bird: Bluebird
State flower: Hawthorn
State tree: Flowering dogwood
Name: The name *Missouri* probably comes from a Native-American word meaning "the one who owns canoes"
Motto: *Salus populi suprema lex esto* ("The welfare of the people shall be the supreme law")
Song: "Missouri Waltz." Words by J. R. Shannon; music by John V. Eppel; arranged by Frederick Knight Logan
State capital: Jefferson City
Population: 5,233,849 (1993); ranked 16th
Total area: 69,709 square miles; ranked 21st
Abbreviation: Mo. (traditional); MO (postal)

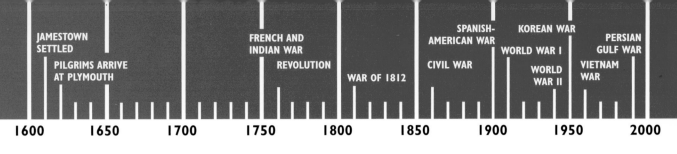

JAMESTOWN SETTLED	FRENCH AND INDIAN WAR	SPANISH-AMERICAN WAR	KOREAN WAR	PERSIAN GULF WAR
PILGRIMS ARRIVE AT PLYMOUTH	REVOLUTION	WORLD WAR I	
	WAR OF 1812	CIVIL WAR	WORLD WAR II	VIETNAM WAR

| 1600 | 1650 | 1700 | 1750 | 1800 | 1850 | 1900 | 1950 | 2000 |

The two great rivers that flow through Missouri—the Mississippi and Missouri—have shaped much of the state's history. The rivers brought explorers to the region and helped it become a center of the fur trade in the 1700s. Later, the rivers brought settlers and Missouri became the starting point for wagon trains heading West. Even today, many of America's products are shipped on these waterways.

The Mississippi River forms Missouri's eastern border. Fields of grass and grain cover the state's rolling northern and western plains. Southern Missouri has forested hills and low mountains. The Missouri Ozarks, in this region, are a popular recreation spot.

Missouri's factories produce airplanes, automobiles, chemicals, and many other products. St.

Louis is the largest city, and Kansas City is famous for its many stockyards. Farming is no longer as important as it once was, but the state produces corn, wheat, cotton, soybeans, and cattle and dairy products.

IMPORTANT DATES

- **1682:** French explorer Sieur de La Salle claims the area of Missouri for France.
- **c. 1735:** Settlers establish Missouri's first permanent white settlement in Ste. Genevieve.
- **1803:** The United States acquires Missouri from France in the Louisiana Purchase.
- **1821:** On August 10, Missouri becomes the 24th state.
- **1861:** Missouri becomes a battleground during the Civil War.
- **1904:** The Louisiana Purchase Exposition is held at St. Louis.
- **1964:** The Gateway Arch, 630 feet high, is opened in St. Louis.
- **1993:** Every county in the state is declared a disaster area after the Mississippi and other rivers flood.

OF SPECIAL INTEREST

- The Wainwright Building in St. Louis, built in 1891, is considered the first American skyscraper.
- The first ice-cream cones were served in 1904 at the Louisiana Purchase Exposition world's fair in St. Louis.
- Gateway Arch, at St. Louis, rises 630 feet alongside the Mississippi River. Inside the stainless-steel arch, trams carry visitors to an observation deck at the top.
- The town of Washington is the world's largest producer of corncob pipes. More than 6 million are produced there each year.

Top: State Capitol, in Jefferson City.
Bottom: The state bird, the bluebird.

MONTANA

TREASURE STATE

A scenic view of Lake McDonald,
at Glacier National Park.

State bird: Western meadowlark
State flower: Bitterroot
State tree: Ponderosa pine
Name: The name *Montana*, of Latin origin,
                          means "mountainous region"
Motto: *Oro y plata* ("Gold and silver")
Song: "Montana." Words by
                          Charles C. Cohan; music
                          by Joseph E. Howard
State capital: Helena
Population: 839,422 (1993); ranked 44th
Total area: 147,046 square miles; ranked 4th
Abbreviation: Mont. (traditional); MT (postal)

JAMESTOWN SETTLED		FRENCH AND INDIAN WAR			SPANISH-AMERICAN WAR	KOREAN WAR	PERSIAN GULF WAR
PILGRIMS ARRIVE AT PLYMOUTH		REVOLUTION				WORLD WAR I	
			WAR OF 1812		CIVIL WAR	WORLD WAR II	VIETNAM WAR

| 1600 | 1650 | 1700 | 1750 | 1800 | 1850 | 1900 | 1950 | 2000 |

Montana has received its name and much of its wealth and beauty from mountains. The Rocky Mountains run through the western part of the state. Years ago, they drew trappers, loggers, and prospectors in search of gold and silver. Today, they draw vacationers. Glacier National Park is one of Montana's most popular attractions. Among the park's scenic mountains are 250 lakes and more than 50 glaciers. Several of the mountain peaks are so steep and jagged that they have never been climbed.

Eastern Montana is very different—a land of flat, broad plains. The vast, uninterrupted view from these plains has given Montana the nickname Big Sky Country. In the southeast, where wind and water have worn away the land, many dinosaur fossils have been found.

More sheep and cattle graze in Montana's vast ranges than in all but a few other states. Montana is also a great wheat- and barley-producing state and a leader in the mining of gold, silver, copper, lead, zinc, and platinum. Montana's eastern plains produce petroleum and have large amounts of coal.

IMPORTANT DATES

• **1803:** The United States acquires eastern Montana from France in the Louisiana Purchase.
• **1805-1806:** Meriwether Lewis and William Clark explore Montana on their way to and from the Pacific.
• **1846:** Western Montana is acquired from Great Britain.
• **1876:** In the Battle of the Little Bighorn, Sioux and other Plains peoples wipe out U.S. troops led by George A. Custer.
• **1889:** On November 8, Montana becomes the 41st state.
• **1951:** Oil wells in the Montana section of the Williston Basin start producing.
• **1960:** Malmstrom Air Force Base becomes the first Minuteman Intercontinental Ballistic Missile site.

OF SPECIAL INTEREST

• More sapphires are found in Montana than in any other state.
• One of the largest gold deposits found in the United States was discovered at Alder Gulch (present-day Virginia City) in 1863.
• Grasshopper Glacier, near Cooke City, contains millions of grasshoppers that became frozen in its ice long ago.
• Giant Springs, in Great Falls, is one of the largest springs in the world. About 300 million gallons of water flow from it each day.

Top: The state flower, bitterroot, in bloom.
Bottom: A thicket of ponderosa pines grows in the Montana wilderness.

57

NEBRASKA

CORNHUSKER STATE

Nebraska's state flower, the goldenrod, flourishes in the wild.

State bird:	Western meadowlark
State flower:	Goldenrod
State tree:	Cottonwood
Name:	The name *Nebraska* comes from the Native-American Oto word *nebrathka*. The word means "shallow" or "spreading water" and was the Oto name for the Platte River
Motto:	"Equality before the law"
Song:	"Beautiful Nebraska." Words by Jim Fras and Guy G. Miller; music by Jim Fras
State capital:	Lincoln
Population:	1,607,199 (1993); ranked 37th
Total area:	77,358 square miles; ranked 16th
Abbreviation:	Neb. (traditional); NE (postal)

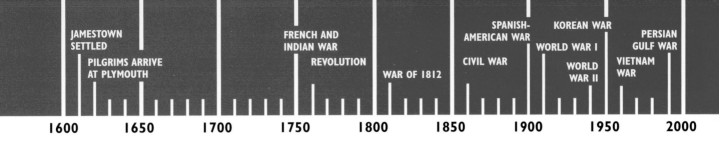

JAMESTOWN SETTLED

PILGRIMS ARRIVE AT PLYMOUTH

FRENCH AND INDIAN WAR

REVOLUTION

WAR OF 1812

SPANISH-AMERICAN WAR

CIVIL WAR

KOREAN WAR

WORLD WAR I

WORLD WAR II

PERSIAN GULF WAR

VIETNAM WAR

1600   1650   1700   1750   1800   1850   1900   1950   2000

In the 1840s, when pioneers passed through the Nebraska region on the Oregon Trail, most thought of it as a desert. But today, irrigation has turned dry, sandy soil into rich cropland. Cattle graze where crops cannot be grown. Farms and ranches now take up more than 92 percent of the state's land, more than any other state.

Nebraska is in the center of the Great Plains. Most of Nebraska is prairie. Near the western border, the High Plains gently rise to an elevation of about one mile above sea level. Nebraska has very cold winters and hot summers. Windstorms, blizzards, and droughts are not uncommon in this state.

Nebraska's rich farmlands produce corn, soybeans, wheat, rye, sorghum, oats, and barley. Corn is the leading crop. Herds of cattle roam the grazing lands. Cattle are also brought to Nebraska to be fattened for market at feed lots. Lincoln, the capital, and Omaha, the largest city, are centers for many financial and insurance companies.

The Oregon Trail, at Scotts Bluff.

IMPORTANT DATES

- **1739:** French explorers Pierre and Paul Mallet are probably the first whites to cross present-day Nebraska.
- **1803:** The United States acquires Nebraska from France in the Louisiana Purchase.
- **1867:** On March 1, Nebraska becomes the 37th state.
- **1877:** The Indian Wars end in Nebraska.
- **1929-1936:** Severe drought creates a dust bowl, destroying crops.
- **1939:** Oil is discovered near Falls City.

OF SPECIAL INTEREST

- The first Cowboy Horse Race took place in Chadron on June 13, 1893.
- The largest mammoth fossil ever found was discovered in 1922 near Wellfleet.
- Nebraska has the largest planted forest in the United States. It covers about 22,000 acres. Arbor Day, a national day for planting trees, originated in Nebraska.
- Lincoln houses the National Museum of Roller Skating, the only such museum in the world.

Top left: Nebraska's state bird, the meadowlark.
Bottom left: State Capitol, in Lincoln.

59

NEVADA

SAGEBRUSH STATE; BATTLE BORN STATE; SILVER STATE

Downtown Las Vegas
lights up in neon at night.

State bird:	Mountain bluebird
State flower:	Sagebrush
State tree:	Single-leaf piñon
Name:	The name *Nevada* comes from a Spanish word meaning "snow-covered"
Motto:	"All for our country"
Song:	"Home Means Nevada." Words and music by Bertha Raffetto
State capital:	Carson City
Population:	1,388,910 (1993); ranked 38th
Total area:	110,567 square miles; ranked 7th
Abbreviation:	Nev. (traditional); NV (postal)

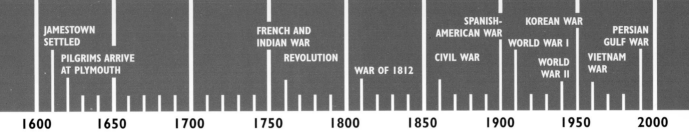

JAMESTOWN SETTLED		FRENCH AND INDIAN WAR			SPANISH-AMERICAN WAR	KOREAN WAR	PERSIAN GULF WAR
PILGRIMS ARRIVE AT PLYMOUTH		REVOLUTION				WORLD WAR I	
			WAR OF 1812	CIVIL WAR		WORLD WAR II	VIETNAM WAR

| 1600 | 1650 | 1700 | 1750 | 1800 | 1850 | 1900 | 1950 | 2000 |

Virginia City and other old mining towns tell the story of Nevada's past. In the 1860s and 1870s, people poured into the region to dig for gold and silver. When the mines ran out, the people left, and boom towns became ghost towns. But today Nevada is growing rapidly again. Visitors come from all over the world to enjoy the hotels and gambling casinos of Las Vegas and the spectacular natural beauty of the state.

Nevada has great extremes in climate. Daytime summer temperatures in some areas often rise above 100°F, with cool nights. Most of Nevada is made up of mountains, valleys, and deserts. The Sierra Nevada mountain range cuts across the southwestern corner of the state. Lake Tahoe, a beautiful glacial lake, is here.

Nevada's main industry is tourism. It accounts for one third of all the jobs in the state. Other important industries manufacture gambling equipment, chemicals, and aerospace products. Nevada's major farm crops include hay, potatoes, and wheat. Cattle and sheep graze on huge ranches in the central and eastern areas of the state.

IMPORTANT DATES

• **1848:** The United States acquires Nevada from Mexico in the Treaty of Guadalupe Hidalgo.
• **1859:** Gold and silver are discovered in the Comstock Lode, near Virginia City, setting off a mining boom.
• **1864:** On October 31, Nevada becomes the 36th state.
• **1931:** The Nevada legislature makes gambling legal in the state.
• **1951:** A series of nuclear tests begins in Nevada. It ends in 1958.
• **1980:** The Nevada legislature passes laws to protect Lake Tahoe from pollution.

OF SPECIAL INTEREST

• The federal government owns about 85 percent of Nevada's land.
• Nevada is the driest of the 50 states, averaging less than four inches of rain a year.
• Hoover Dam, on the Colorado River, southeast of Las Vegas, is one of the world's largest concrete dams. It forms Lake Mead, the largest human-made lake in the United States.
• In Great Basin National Park, in east-central Nevada, 3,000-year-old bristlecone pines grow.

Top: An old bristlecone pine tree at Great Basin National Park.
Bottom: Skiing at Lake Tahoe.

NEW HAMPSHIRE

GRANITE STATE

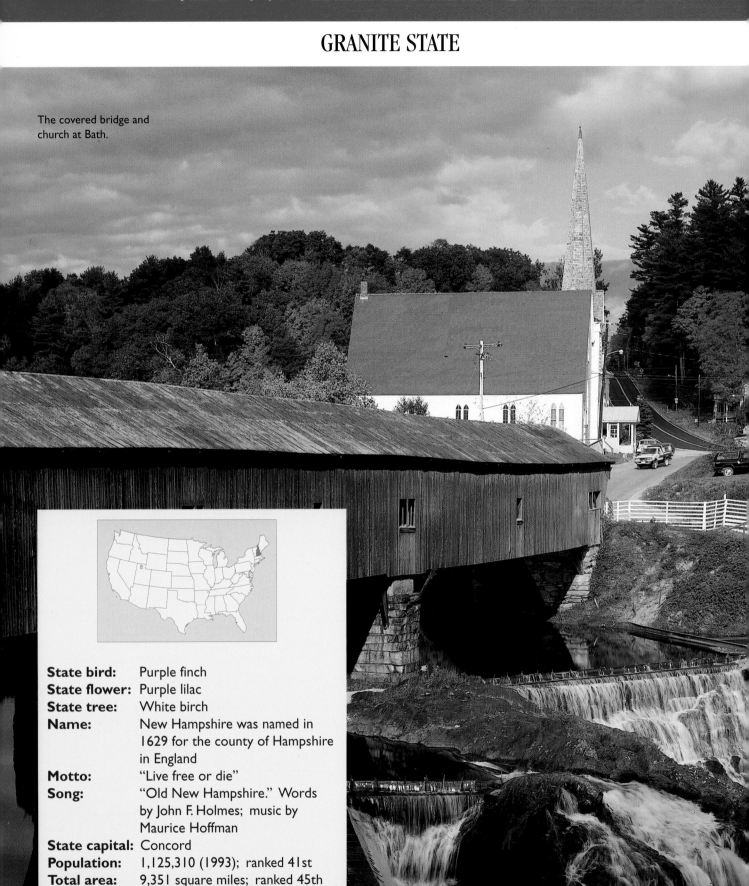

The covered bridge and church at Bath.

State bird:	Purple finch
State flower:	Purple lilac
State tree:	White birch
Name:	New Hampshire was named in 1629 for the county of Hampshire in England
Motto:	"Live free or die"
Song:	"Old New Hampshire." Words by John F. Holmes; music by Maurice Hoffman
State capital:	Concord
Population:	1,125,310 (1993); ranked 41st
Total area:	9,351 square miles; ranked 45th
Abbreviation:	N.H. (traditional); NH (postal)

JAMESTOWN SETTLED		FRENCH AND INDIAN WAR			SPANISH-AMERICAN WAR	KOREAN WAR		PERSIAN GULF WAR
PILGRIMS ARRIVE AT PLYMOUTH		REVOLUTION			WORLD WAR I		VIETNAM WAR
			WAR OF 1812	CIVIL WAR		WORLD WAR II	

| 1600 | 1650 | 1700 | 1750 | 1800 | 1850 | 1900 | 1950 | 2000 |

New Hampshire is well known for its beauty and year-round attractions. Its mountains draw many climbers and skiers. More than 1,300 lakes, streams, and ponds provide opportunities for fishing, swimming, and boating. In the fall, the New Hampshire foliage is ablaze with autumn colors.

Along New Hampshire's northern border are the White Mountains. Mount Washington, the highest peak in the Northeast (6,288 feet above sea level), is located there. It is one of the windiest and coldest places in the world. The state's western border is formed by the Connecticut River. More than 80 percent of New Hampshire's land is covered by forest.

Tourism and manufacturing are New Hampshire's leading industries. The state's forests provide the raw materials for producing lumber, pulp, and paper. New Hampshire also grows many Christmas trees. The state's factories make machinery, plastics, and metal products. New Hampshire also mines granite, a stone used in making buildings. New Hampshire granite was used to make the main building for the United Nations in New York City.

IMPORTANT DATES

• **1603:** English explorer Martin Pring sails up the Piscataqua River.
• **1623:** David Thompson founds the first European settlement, near present-day Portsmouth.
• **1788:** On June 21, New Hampshire becomes the 9th state.
• **1838:** The first railroad in the state is completed.
• **1944:** The United Nations (UN) Monetary and Financial Conference is held at Bretton Woods. It creates an international fund and bank.
• **1964:** New Hampshire legalizes the first state lottery since the 1890s.

OF SPECIAL INTEREST

• The Brattle organ in St. John's Episcopal Church in Portsmouth is believed to be the oldest pipe organ in the United States. It dates back to 1708.
• The oldest publicly funded library in the United States is located at Peterborough. It was founded in 1833.
• In the 1800s, Concord produced stagecoaches that were used throughout the world. Concord coaches were famous for their detailed construction.
• Old Man of the Mountain is a rock formation on Profile Mountain. It looks like the side of an old man's face and is about 40 feet high.

Top: New Hampshire's state bird, the purple finch.
Bottom: A scenic view of Marlow.

NEW JERSEY

GARDEN STATE

The sandy shoreline at
Island Beach State Park.

State bird:	Eastern goldfinch
State flower:	Purple violet
State tree:	Red oak
Name:	New Jersey was named after England's Isle of Jersey
Motto:	"Liberty and prosperity"
Song:	None
State capital:	Trenton
Population:	7,879,164 (1993); ranked 9th
Total area:	8,722 square miles; ranked 46th
Abbreviation:	N.J. (traditional); NJ (postal)

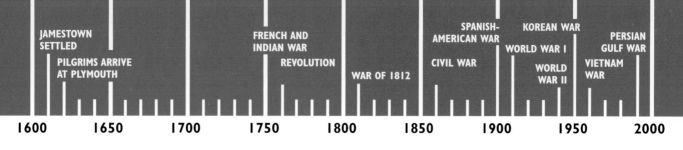

JAMESTOWN SETTLED	FRENCH AND INDIAN WAR	SPANISH-AMERICAN WAR	KOREAN WAR	PERSIAN GULF WAR
PILGRIMS ARRIVE AT PLYMOUTH	REVOLUTION	WORLD WAR I	VIETNAM WAR
	WAR OF 1812	CIVIL WAR	WORLD WAR II

1600   1650   1700   1750   1800   1850   1900   1950   2000

New Jersey is one of the smallest states, but it has one of the largest populations. Nearly all of its people live in cities or towns, but New Jersey is also a state of beautiful beaches and summer resorts. More than 50 resorts, including Asbury Park and Atlantic City, are scattered along its Atlantic coast.

New Jersey is surrounded by water on all sides, except for the 50-mile border that it shares with the state of New York. The Atlantic Ocean and Hudson River are on its eastern border. The Delaware River serves as the state's western border. Delaware Bay is to the southwest. The southern part of New Jersey is covered in gently rolling plains. Pine forests, natural meadows, and salt marshes cover a great deal of New Jersey's Atlantic coastline. The Appalachian Mountains run across the northwestern corner of the state.

New Jersey ranks among the top ten states in manufacturing. Its factories produce medical drugs, electric and electronic equipment, chemicals, petroleum products, and printed materials. New Jersey farms grow potatoes, tomatoes, corn, lettuce, cranberries, blueberries, and peaches.

IMPORTANT DATES
• **1524:** Italian navigator Giovanni da Verrazano explores the New Jersey coast.
• **1618:** The Dutch establish a trading post colony at Bergen, part of present-day Jersey City.
• **1778:** General George Washington defeats the British at Monmouth during the Revolution.
• **1787:** On December 18, New Jersey becomes the 3rd state.
• **1927:** The Holland Tunnel opens, connecting New Jersey and New York City.
• **1978:** New Jersey voters approve legalized gambling in Atlantic City.

OF SPECIAL INTEREST
• The first organized baseball game was held in Hoboken in 1846. The New York Nine beat the New York Knickerbockers, 23 to 1.
• The first dinosaur skeleton discovered in North America was found in Haddonfield in 1858.
• The first intercollegiate football game was held in New Brunswick in 1869. Rutgers University defeated Princeton, 6 to 4.
• Thomas Edison developed his electric light at Menlo Park in 1879.

Top: New Jersey's gambling center, Atlantic City.
Bottom: Vacationers relax in Pinelands.

NEW MEXICO

LAND OF ENCHANTMENT

The white sands of New Mexico's vast desert area.

State bird:	Roadrunner
State flower:	Yucca flower
State tree:	Piñon (nut pine)
Name:	The Spanish named New Mexico for Mexico, which took its name from an Aztec war god
Motto:	*Crescit eundo* ("It grows as it goes")
Song:	"O, Fair New Mexico." Words and music by Elizabeth Garrett
State capital:	Santa Fe
Population:	1,616,483 (1993); ranked 36th
Total area:	121,598 square miles; ranked 5th
Abbreviation:	N. Mex. (traditional); NM (postal)

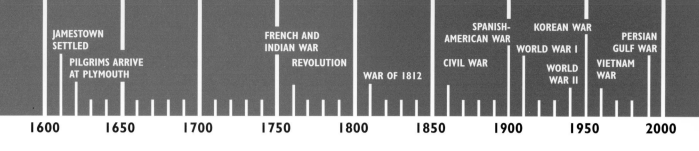

JAMESTOWN SETTLED	FRENCH AND INDIAN WAR	SPANISH-AMERICAN WAR	KOREAN WAR	PERSIAN GULF WAR
PILGRIMS ARRIVE AT PLYMOUTH	REVOLUTION	CIVIL WAR	WORLD WAR I	VIETNAM WAR
	WAR OF 1812		WORLD WAR II	

| 1600 | 1650 | 1700 | 1750 | 1800 | 1850 | 1900 | 1950 | 2000 |

New Mexico is a land of mountains, canyons, deserts, caves, plateaus, and flat-topped hills called mesas. This rugged scenery and a warm, sunny climate attract millions of visitors each year. The eastern third of New Mexico is covered with great, rolling plains. The mighty Rocky Mountains extend into the north-central part of the state. Scattered mountain ranges south and west of the Rockies are separated by deserts. Northwestern New Mexico is made up of valleys and plains, canyons, rugged cliffs, and mesas.

Santa Fe and Taos are cities steeped in history and are today cultural centers. Descendants of New Mexico's first people, Native Americans, still live in the state, as do descendants of the Spanish and Mexicans who controlled the region for 300 years.

New Mexico is a leading mining state, with major deposits of coal, copper, silver, iron, potash, and aluminum. Natural gas and petroleum are important products. Cattle ranching is the chief kind of farming in the state. Irrigated land produces cotton, sorghum, hay, onions, wheat, and pecans.

Left: Carlsbad Caverns.

IMPORTANT DATES

- **1540:** Francisco Vásquez de Coronado of Spain begins the European exploration and conquest of New Mexico.
- **1598:** Juan de Oñate claims New Mexico for Spain and founds the first permanent Spanish settlement in the state.
- **1821:** New Mexico becomes a province of Mexico.
- **1848:** Mexico gives up New Mexico to the United States in a treaty ending the Mexican War.
- **1912:** On January 6, New Mexico becomes the 47th state.
- **1945:** The world's first atomic bomb is tested near Alamogordo.
- **1985:** New Mexico is plagued by record numbers of grasshoppers.
- **1988:** Severe drought hits the state.

OF SPECIAL INTEREST

- Pueblo Bonito was built by Native Americans of the Anasazi tribe more than 1,200 years ago.
- El Camino Real is the oldest road made by Europeans in the United States. Travelers started using it around 1581. It stretched from Sante Fe to Mexico City, Mexico.
- The Palace of Governors in Santa Fe is the oldest government building in the United States. It was built in 1609-1610. Santa Fe is the oldest state capital in the United States.
- New Mexico is the only state with two official languages—English and Spanish.
- The largest known underground chambers are located at Carlsbad Caverns National Park.
- White Sands Missile Range, in south-central New Mexico, is the largest all-land rocket-testing range in the United States.

67

NEW YORK

EMPIRE STATE

A view across the East River encompasses the Brooklyn Bridge and the World Trade Towers.

State bird: Bluebird
State flower: Rose
State tree: Sugar maple
Name: New York was named after the Duke of York of England
Motto: *Excelsior* ("Ever upward")
Song: "I Love New York." Words and music by Steve Karmen
State capital: Albany
Population: 18,197,154 (1993); ranked 2nd
Total area: 54,471 square miles; ranked 27th
Abbreviation: N.Y. (traditional); NY (postal)

JAMESTOWN SETTLED

PILGRIMS ARRIVE AT PLYMOUTH

FRENCH AND INDIAN WAR

REVOLUTION

WAR OF 1812

SPANISH-AMERICAN WAR

CIVIL WAR

KOREAN WAR

WORLD WAR I

WORLD WAR II

PERSIAN GULF WAR

VIETNAM WAR

1600   1650   1700   1750   1800   1850   1900   1950   2000

New York State is the home of the largest city in the United States, New York City. It is the leading financial and business center of the nation. But New York has much to offer beyond the city. Its varied landscape is covered with wooded hills and clear lakes. Niagara Falls, the Hudson River Valley, the beaches of Long Island, and the Catskill and Adirondack Mountains are all popular vacation spots.

The Adirondacks cover much of northern New York. South of these mountains, the Appalachian Plateau spreads out over half the state; within this region are the Catskills. The Hudson River rises in the Adirondacks and flows more than 300 miles to the Atlantic. Long Island stretches 120 miles eastward from the mouth of the Hudson into the Atlantic.

New York City's theaters, museums, and concert halls make it a leading cultural center. It is also an important business city and one of the world's busiest seaports. Farming, especially dairy farming, is import-

ant in central and western New York. The state's factories manufacture many products, including printed materials, scientific instruments, machinery, drugs, soaps, chemicals, paints, and plastics. New York leads all states in the production of clothing.

IMPORTANT DATES

• **1524:** Italian navigator Giovanni da Verrazano sails into New York Bay.
• **1609:** England's Henry Hudson explores the Hudson River Valley.
• **1624:** The Dutch found the first permanent settlement at Fort Orange (now Albany). They call the region New Netherland.
• **1626:** Peter Minuit buys Manhattan from local Native Americans.
• **1788:** On July 26, New York becomes the 11th state. New York City is the first U.S. capital.
• **1825:** The Erie Canal opens, linking the Hudson River and the Great Lakes.
• **1886:** The Statue of Liberty is dedicated.
• **1931:** The Empire State Building is completed in New York City.
• **1973:** The World Trade Center is dedicated in New York City.
• **1980:** The Winter Olympic Games are held at Lake Placid, which was also the site for the 1932 Winter Games.

OF SPECIAL INTEREST

• The national symbol known as Uncle Sam originated in Troy in the early 1800s.
• The first escalator was manufactured in 1899 by the Otis Elevator Company in New York City.
• Radio City Music Hall in New York City is the world's largest indoor theater, seating 5,900.
• The World Trade Center in New York City has the world's second-tallest skyscrapers.
• The National Baseball Hall of Fame is located in Cooperstown.

Top: The Statue of Liberty.
Bottom: Niagara Falls.

NORTH CAROLINA

TAR HEEL STATE; OLD NORTH STATE

Cape Lookout Lighthouse, on the Outer Banks.

State bird: Cardinal
State flower: Flowering dogwood
State tree: Pine
Name: North Carolina was named for Charles I of England
Motto: *Esse quam videri* ("To be, rather than to seem")
Song: "The Old North State." Words and music by William Gaston
State capital: Raleigh
Population: 6,945,180 (1993); ranked 10th
Total area: 53,821 square miles; ranked 28th
Abbreviation: N.C. (traditional); NC (postal)

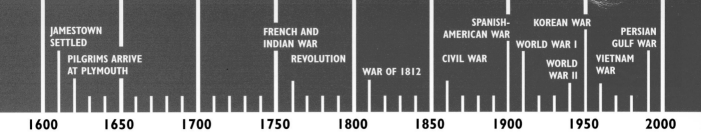

JAMESTOWN SETTLED		FRENCH AND INDIAN WAR				SPANISH-AMERICAN WAR	KOREAN WAR		PERSIAN GULF WAR
PILGRIMS ARRIVE AT PLYMOUTH		REVOLUTION			CIVIL WAR	WORLD WAR I		VIETNAM WAR
			WAR OF 1812			WORLD WAR II	

1600   1650   1700   1750   1800   1850   1900   1950   2000

North Carolina's long Atlantic Ocean coastline has many inlets, islands, and reefs. A string of barrier islands, the Outer Banks, meets the ocean along much of the coast. Rough seas and unpredictable currents make these shores some of the most dangerous in the world. Many ships have been wrecked along them, especially off Cape Hatteras, an area called the Graveyard of the Atlantic.

West of the coast, plains provide fertile land for growing crops. Farther west, the land rises in rolling, wooded hills and valleys. The far western part of North Carolina is covered with rugged mountains. The Blue Ridge, Great Smoky, and other ranges of the Appalachian Mountains provide much spectacular scenery.

Fabric and furniture are two of North Carolina's most important products. Most of the nation's homes have some furniture made in North Carolina. North Carolina is the leading state in tobacco farming. Its rich farmland also produces such crops as sweet potatoes, soybeans, corn, and peanuts.

IMPORTANT DATES
- **1524:** Italian navigator Giovanni da Verrazano explores the North Carolina coast.
- **1585:** The first English colony in America is established at Roanoke Island.
- **1712:** Carolina is divided into two provinces.
- **1789:** On November 21, North Carolina becomes the 12th state.
- **1861:** North Carolina joins the Confederacy in the Civil War.
- **1903:** The Wright brothers make the first successful airplane flight near Kitty Hawk.
- **1966:** Cape Lookout National Seashore is established.

OF SPECIAL INTEREST
- Virginia Dare was the first English child born in America. She was born on Roanoke Island on August 18, 1587. Virginia and the other colonists disappeared without a trace, and the "Lost Colony" of Roanoke remains one of the great mysteries of history.
- Ocracoke Island was a hideout for Blackbeard the pirate. It is located about 20 miles off the shore of North Carolina.

Top: State Capitol Building, in Raleigh.
Bottom: A historical re-enactment at Bentonville Battleground.

NORTH DAKOTA

PEACE GARDEN STATE

Bright sunflowers fill a
North Dakota field.

State bird: Western meadowlark

State flower: Wild prairie rose

State tree: American elm

Name: North Dakota was named for the Dakota Sioux, who lived in the area before white people arrived. *Dakota* means "allies"

Motto: "Liberty and union, now and forever, one and inseparable"

Song: "North Dakota Hymn." Words by James W. Foley; music by C. S. Putnam

State capital: Bismarck

Population: 634,935 (1993); ranked 47th

Total area: 70,704 square miles; ranked 19th

Abbreviation: N. Dak. (traditional); ND (postal)

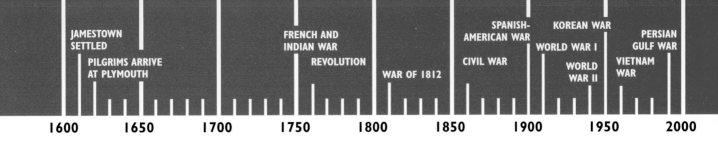

JAMESTOWN SETTLED		FRENCH AND INDIAN WAR			SPANISH-AMERICAN WAR	KOREAN WAR		PERSIAN GULF WAR
PILGRIMS ARRIVE AT PLYMOUTH		REVOLUTION				WORLD WAR I		VIETNAM WAR
			WAR OF 1812	CIVIL WAR		WORLD WAR II		

1600   1650   1700   1750   1800   1850   1900   1950   2000

North Dakota was one of the last regions of the American frontier to be settled. Even today, it has a small population. Still, North Dakota is a major farming state. Its economy relies more heavily on farming than any other state except South Dakota. More than half the people in North Dakota live in rural areas, and the state has more farm workers than any other state.

In the eastern half of North Dakota, level prairies stretch as far as the eye can see. The land gradually rises across the state to the high plateaus of the west. In the southwest are the Badlands, a region where wind and water have carved strange formations into the soft, light sandstone rock.

The Sioux and other Native Americans once hunted bison on North Dakota's open plains. Today, most of North Dakota is covered by large farms and ranches.

The average farm is about 1,000 acres in size. The chief crop is wheat, but North Dakota is also an important producer of other grains, sugar beets, sunflowers, and cattle. Western North Dakota has deposits of coal, petroleum, and natural gas.

IMPORTANT DATES
• **1738:** French fur trader Pierre Gaultier de Varennes, Sieur de La Vérendrye, is the first European to explore North Dakota.
• **1803:** The United States acquires southwestern North Dakota from France in the Louisiana Purchase.
• **1812:** The first permanent white settlement is established at Pembina.
• **1818:** The United States acquires part of North Dakota from Great Britain.
• **1889:** On November 2, North Dakota becomes the 39th state.
• **1929-1936:** A major drought hits the state.
• **1951:** Oil is discovered at Williston Basin near Tioga.
• **1988:** A major drought and heat wave cause damage to 3.5 million acres.

OF SPECIAL INTEREST
• Portal is the site of an international golf course. Part of the course is in the United States, and part is in Canada.
• Only four cities in North Dakota have a population of more than 25,000. Fargo is the largest, with a population of about 74,000.
• At Burning Coal Mine, coal has been burning underground for several hundred years.

Top: State Capitol, in Bismarck.
Bottom: North Dakota's state flower, the wild prairie rose.

OHIO

BUCKEYE STATE

The Conservatory at
Franklin Park, in Columbus.

State bird: Cardinal
State flower: Scarlet carnation
State tree: Buckeye
Name: Ohio took its name from the Iroquois word meaning "good river"
Motto: "With God all things are possible"
Song: "Beautiful Ohio." Words by Ballard MacDonald; music by Mary Earl
State capital: Columbus
Population: 11,091,301 (1993); ranked 7th
Total area: 44,828 square miles; ranked 34th
Abbreviation: O. (traditional); OH (postal)

JAMESTOWN SETTLED			FRENCH AND INDIAN WAR				SPANISH-AMERICAN WAR	KOREAN WAR		PERSIAN GULF WAR

PILGRIMS ARRIVE AT PLYMOUTH   REVOLUTION   WAR OF 1812   CIVIL WAR   WORLD WAR I   WORLD WAR II   VIETNAM WAR

1600   1650   1700   1750   1800   1850   1900   1950   2000

Ohio has more industries than almost any other state. Machine tools, tires, steel, petroleum, automobiles, plastics, chemicals, and many other products are turned out by Ohio factories. Dayton is one of the aviation centers of the world. The Wright brothers first experimented with flying machines there, and today it is the site of Wright-Patterson Air Force Base, the nation's largest air force research field. Visitors to the base can tour the U.S. Air Force Museum.

Most of northern Ohio lies along the shores of Lake Erie. The land along the lake is mostly plains, broken by a few low, sandy ridges. Most of western Ohio is part of the rich Midwestern Corn Belt, made up of plains and gently rolling hills. Rolling hills and valleys in the eastern half of the state create beautiful scenery in Ohio. This region includes the state's largest forests.

Industry is the backbone of Ohio's economy, but 60 percent of the land is used for farming. Major crops are corn, soybeans, oats, tomatoes, hay, and wheat.

Some tobacco is grown in the southern part of the state, and fruit farms dot the banks of the Ohio River.

IMPORTANT DATES

• **1669:** French explorer Sieur de La Salle explores the Ohio region.
• **1788:** The first permanent white settlement in Ohio is set up at Marietta.
• **1803:** On March 1, Ohio becomes the 17th state.
• **1870:** Standard Oil Company is organized at Cleveland.
• **1913:** Floods in the Miami River Valley cause enormous destruction.
• **1967:** Carl B. Stokes is elected mayor of Cleveland, becoming the first African-American mayor of a major U.S. city.
• **1980:** A long-running border dispute with Kentucky is settled in Ohio's favor.

OF SPECIAL INTEREST

• Oberlin College was the first U.S. college for both men and women, established in 1837.
• The first public weather-forecasting service in the country began in Cincinnati in 1869.
• The Cincinnati Red Stockings (now known as the Cincinnati Reds) became the first professional baseball team in 1869.
• Serpent Mound, in southern Ohio, was built by prehistoric Native Americans, the Adenas, some 2,000 years ago. It is a huge mound, more than 1,000 feet long, in the shape of a snake holding an egg in its mouth.
• The Pro Football Hall of Fame is located in Canton.

Top: Columbus's German Village.
Bottom: Fourth of July on the banks of the Ohio.

75

OKLAHOMA

SOONER STATE

The State Capitol, in Oklahoma City, is the only capitol with oil-producing wells on its grounds.

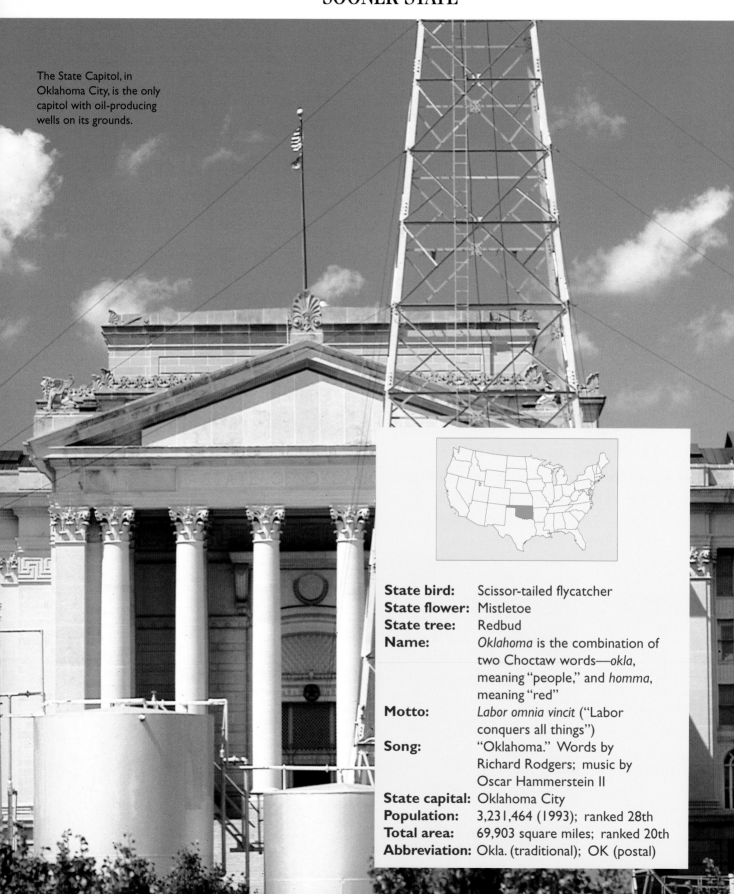

State bird:	Scissor-tailed flycatcher
State flower:	Mistletoe
State tree:	Redbud
Name:	*Oklahoma* is the combination of two Choctaw words—*okla*, meaning "people," and *homma*, meaning "red"
Motto:	*Labor omnia vincit* ("Labor conquers all things")
Song:	"Oklahoma." Words by Richard Rodgers; music by Oscar Hammerstein II
State capital:	Oklahoma City
Population:	3,231,464 (1993); ranked 28th
Total area:	69,903 square miles; ranked 20th
Abbreviation:	Okla. (traditional); OK (postal)

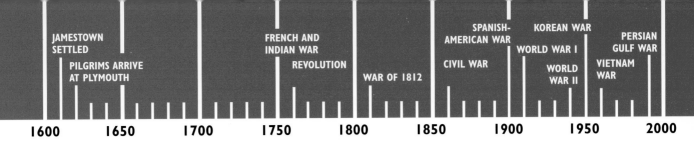

JAMESTOWN SETTLED

PILGRIMS ARRIVE AT PLYMOUTH

FRENCH AND INDIAN WAR

REVOLUTION

WAR OF 1812

SPANISH-AMERICAN WAR

CIVIL WAR

KOREAN WAR

WORLD WAR I

WORLD WAR II

VIETNAM WAR

PERSIAN GULF WAR

1600   1650   1700   1750   1800   1850   1900   1950   2000

Dinosaurs walked across the Oklahoma region more than 200 million years ago, leaving footprints that are preserved as fossils. Elaborate carvings on canyon walls along the Cimarron River were made by Native Americans more than 10,000 years ago. In the late 1800s, white settlers began to flood into the state. Despite this land rush, today Oklahoma has the highest Native-American population of any state.

Most of Oklahoma's land is gently rolling prairie broken by mountain ranges. The Quachita Mountains rise along the southeastern border. The Arbuckle Mountains are located in the south-central part of the state. Rugged, flat mesas rise in the Oklahoma Panhandle, the long narrow strip of land that makes up the northwestern part of the state.

Oklahoma is a major producer of oil and natural gas. The state's factories turn out machinery, plastics, and other products. Farms grow wheat, cotton, and other crops. Beef cattle, raised on large ranches, are the most important farm product.

IMPORTANT DATES

- **1541:** Spanish explorer Francisco Vásquez de Coronado crosses western Oklahoma.
- **1682:** French explorer Sieur de La Salle claims Oklahoma for France.
- **1803:** The United States acquires most of Oklahoma from France in the Louisiana Purchase.
- **1834:** Oklahoma is officially designated Indian Territory.
- **1889:** Parts of Oklahoma are opened to white settlement, creating a land rush.
- **1897:** Oklahoma's first commercial oil well is drilled at Bartlesville.
- **1907:** On November 16, Oklahoma becomes the 46th state.
- **1930s:** Drought and dust storms force farmers into bankruptcy. Many people move west in search of work.
- **1965:** The National Cowboy Hall of Fame is opened in Oklahoma City.
- **1995:** A bomb destroys the federal office building in Oklahoma City, in the worst terrorist attack in U.S. history.

OF SPECIAL INTEREST

- On the morning of April 22, 1889, the region around present-day Oklahoma City was an empty prairie. That day, the region was opened to white settlement, and by nightfall, it had a population of more than 10,000.
- Oklahoma's people include members of more than 60 Native-American tribes.

Top: Cooking at a chuckwagon gathering at the Cowboy Hall of Fame.
Bottom: A dancer performs at the American Indian Exposition in Anadarko.

OREGON

BEAVER STATE

A scenic view of
Tillamook County.

State bird:	Western meadowlark
State flower:	Oregon grape
State tree:	Douglas fir
Name:	The name *Oregon* is from the French word *ouragan*, which means "hurricane"
Motto:	"The union"
Song:	"Oregon, My Oregon." Words by J.A. Buchanan; music by Henry B. Murtagh
State capital:	Salem
Population:	3,031,867 (1993); ranked 29th
Total area:	98,386 square miles; ranked 9th
Abbreviation:	Ore. (traditional); OR (postal)

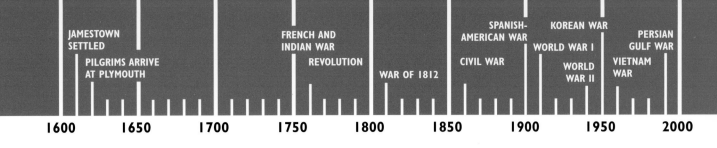

JAMESTOWN SETTLED			FRENCH AND INDIAN WAR			SPANISH-AMERICAN WAR	KOREAN WAR	PERSIAN GULF WAR
PILGRIMS ARRIVE AT PLYMOUTH			REVOLUTION		WAR OF 1812	CIVIL WAR	WORLD WAR I	VIETNAM WAR
							WORLD WAR II	

1600   1650   1700   1750   1800   1850   1900   1950   2000

In the 1840s and 1850s, covered wagons carried thousands of pioneers west to Oregon. The state is still attracting people today, new residents and visitors alike. One reason is the state's spectacular scenery—its rugged coast, tall mountains, forests, waterfalls, lakes, and rivers.

Steep cliffs rise along much of the Oregon coast. But sandy beaches and protected harbors are also part of the coastline. The Cascade Mountains, with their snow-covered volcanic peaks, rise west of the coast. The eastern half of the state is covered by the Columbia Plateau. Deep river canyons cut through part of the plateau, and much of the area is rugged and mountainous. The Pacific Ocean brings rain and mild temperatures to the coast. Eastern sections of the state are drier, and temperatures vary more.

Oregon's vast forests make lumber its most important product. Cattle are raised in the east. The state's crops include wheat, potatoes, winter pears, blackberries, and many vegetables. The Willamette Valley is famous for its orchards and wine grapes. Portland is an important West Coast port.

IMPORTANT DATES
• **1542:** Spanish explorer Bartolomé Ferrelo probably sails along the Oregon coast.
• **1792:** American explorer Robert Gray sails to the mouth of the Columbia River.
• **1811:** John Jacob Astor founds Fort Astoria, the first white settlement in the region.
• **1819:** A treaty between the United States and Spain fixes the southern border of Oregon.
• **1846:** A treaty with Great Britain gives the United States control of the Oregon territory.
• **1859:** On February 14, Oregon becomes the 33rd state.
• **1883:** Railroad lines link Oregon with the eastern United States.
• **1937:** Bonneville Dam, on the Columbia River, is completed.
• **1967:** Astoria Bridge opens, linking Oregon and Washington.

OF SPECIAL INTEREST
• Crater Lake, in Oregon's Cascade Mountains, is nearly 2,000 feet deep—the deepest lake in the United States.
• At one time, so many beaver pelts were taken in Oregon that they were used as money.
• Mills Ends Park is the world's smallest official park. It is about 19 inches across and 24 inches long. It is located on a traffic island in Portland. The park was created on St. Patrick's Day in 1948, as a colony for leprechauns and a place for snail races.
• Oregon cuts more lumber and produces more forest products than any other state.

Top: A ghost town in Waterman.
Bottom: Natural beauty at Green Lakes Basin.

PENNSYLVANIA

KEYSTONE STATE

State bird: Ruffed grouse
State flower: Mountain laurel
State tree: Hemlock
Name: The name *Pennsylvania* means "Penn's Woods." The state was named in honor of founder William Penn's father.
Motto: "Virtue, liberty, and independence"
Song: None
State capital: Harrisburg
Population: 12,048,271 (1993); ranked 5th
Total area: 45,308 square miles; ranked 33rd
Abbreviation: Penn. (traditional); PA (postal)

An Amish family travels down a Pennsylvania road in a horse-drawn buggy.

JAMESTOWN SETTLED		FRENCH AND INDIAN WAR			SPANISH-AMERICAN WAR	KOREAN WAR	PERSIAN GULF WAR
PILGRIMS ARRIVE AT PLYMOUTH		REVOLUTION			WORLD WAR I		VIETNAM WAR
			WAR OF 1812	CIVIL WAR		WORLD WAR II	

| 1600 | 1650 | 1700 | 1750 | 1800 | 1850 | 1900 | 1950 | 2000 |

Pennsylvania holds a special place in American history. The Declaration of Independence and the U.S. Constitution were both drawn up in Philadelphia, at Independence Hall. One of the most famous and bloody battles of the Civil War was fought in the state, at Gettysburg. These and other events are remembered at historic sites across the state.

Rolling hills, gently sloping valleys, and low plateaus make up most of Pennsylvania. The Delaware River forms its eastern border, while the northwest corner of the state borders on Lake Erie. Forests cover about half of Pennsylvania. The Pocono Mountains, in the northeast, are a popular vacation spot. The Allegheny Mountains, in south-central Pennsylvania, have extensive deposits of anthracite (hard) coal.

Steel and iron have been important products since the late 1800s, especially around Pittsburgh. The state also produces automobiles, glass, ceramic items, chemicals, and food products, especially chocolates. Many large dairy farms are located in eastern Pennsylvania; the soil along Lake Erie is ideal for farming.

IMPORTANT DATES

• **1615:** French explorer Étienne Brûlé travels down the Susquehanna River.
• **1643:** Swedish settlers found a fort on Tinicum Island, the first permanent settlement in Pennsylvania.
• **1681:** King Charles II of England gives Pennsylvania to William Penn.
• **1776:** The Declaration of Independence is adopted in Philadelphia.
• **1787:** On December 12, Pennsylvania becomes the 2nd state. The U.S. Constitution is drawn up in Philadelphia.
• **1859:** Edwin Drake drills the first oil well in the United States near Titusville.
• **1863:** President Abraham Lincoln delivers the "Gettysburg Address" at Gettysburg.
• **1889:** Johnstown is destroyed by flood in one of the worst disasters in U.S. history.
• **1979:** A nuclear power plant accident at Three Mile Island releases radioactive gases.

OF SPECIAL INTEREST

• The Pennsylvania Dutch—descendants of German settlers—live simply, according to their religious beliefs. Many do not drive cars or use telephones or electricity.
• The first department store was opened by John Wanamaker in Philadelphia in the 1870s.
• The ice-cream soda was invented by Robert M. Green in Philadelphia in 1874.
• The Hershey plant, in Hershey, is the world's largest chocolate factory, established in 1905.

Top: Philadelphia's historic Independence Hall.
Bottom: Pennsylvania's state flower, the mountain laurel.

81

RHODE ISLAND

LITTLE RHODY; OCEAN STATE

A stream flows past Wilkinson and Slater Mill Historic site in Pawtucket.

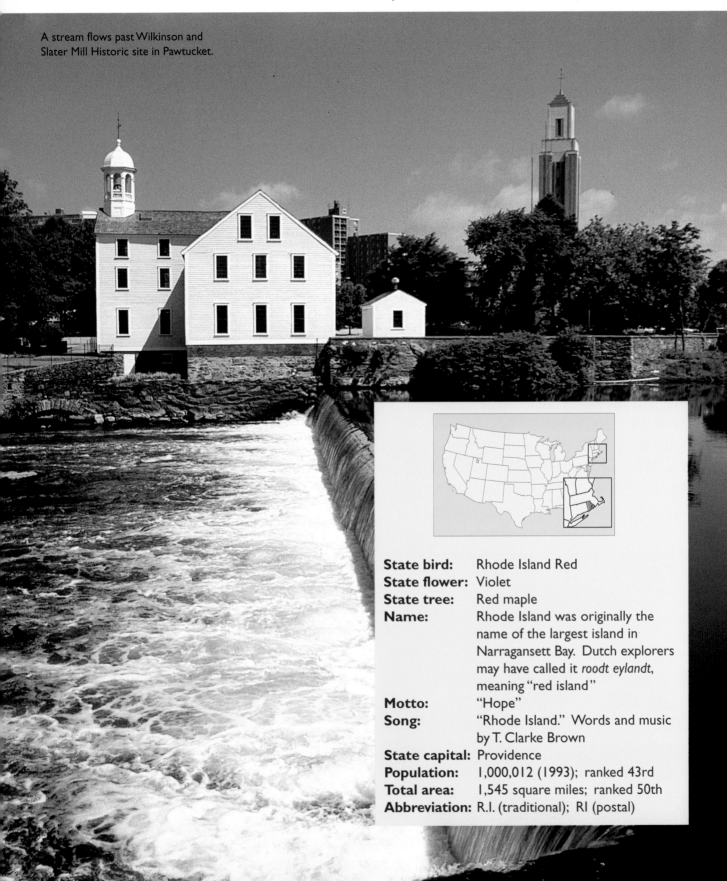

State bird:	Rhode Island Red
State flower:	Violet
State tree:	Red maple
Name:	Rhode Island was originally the name of the largest island in Narragansett Bay. Dutch explorers may have called it *roodt eylandt*, meaning "red island"
Motto:	"Hope"
Song:	"Rhode Island." Words and music by T. Clarke Brown
State capital:	Providence
Population:	1,000,012 (1993); ranked 43rd
Total area:	1,545 square miles; ranked 50th
Abbreviation:	R.I. (traditional); RI (postal)

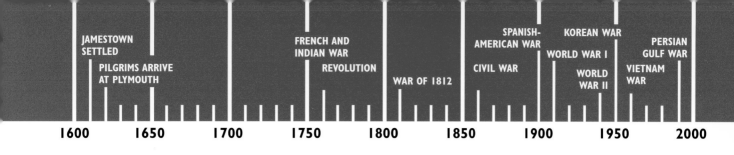

JAMESTOWN SETTLED		FRENCH AND INDIAN WAR		SPANISH-AMERICAN WAR	KOREAN WAR	PERSIAN GULF WAR	
PILGRIMS ARRIVE AT PLYMOUTH		REVOLUTION		WORLD WAR I			
			WAR OF 1812	CIVIL WAR	WORLD WAR II	VIETNAM WAR	

1600   1650   1700   1750   1800   1850   1900   1950   2000

Rhode Island is the nation's smallest state, but Narragansett Bay has given it an especially long coastline. The scenic beauty of the bay and its many cozy islands have made it a popular vacation spot. Providence, the state's largest city, is the second-largest city in New England—only Boston is larger. Four fifths of Rhode Island's population live in Providence and surrounding towns.

Sandy beaches and rocky cliffs line Rhode Island's shores. Inland and to the west, the land rises gradually to form forested slopes. Many lakes and ponds nestle among the low hills.

Rhode Island is an important industrial state. Its many factories turn out textiles, machinery, toys, chemicals, plastics, electrical equipment, silverware,

and costume jewelry. The state's farms produce nursery and greenhouse goods, potatoes, corn, apples, and peaches. Poultry farms provide chickens, eggs, and turkeys. Fishing is one of the state's oldest industries.

IMPORTANT DATES

• **1524:** Italian explorer Giovanni da Verrazano, sailing for France, reaches Narragansett Bay.
• **1636:** Roger Williams founds Providence after fleeing from religious persecution in Massachusetts.
• **1776:** Rhode Island is the first colony to declare its independence from England.
• **1790:** On May 29, Rhode Island becomes the 13th state.
• **1900:** Providence becomes the state capital.
• **1938:** A hurricane and tidal wave strike, causing one of the state's worst natural disasters.
• **1978:** The Narragansett tribe wins a claim to land in Charlestown.

OF SPECIAL INTEREST

• Rhode Island is the smallest of all the states.
• Samuel Slater built America's first successful waterpower textile mill at Pawtucket in 1790.
• Newport is a famous summer resort. Mansions built in the late 1800s and early 1900s are now a major tourist attraction.
• The oldest Jewish synagogue in the United States is located at Newport. It was built in 1763.
• The Rhode Island Red, a breed of chicken, made poultry raising a major U.S. industry.

Top: The Breakers is one of Newport's most stately mansions.
Bottom: Sailing is a popular attraction for Rhode Island's residents and visitors.

SOUTH CAROLINA

PALMETTO STATE

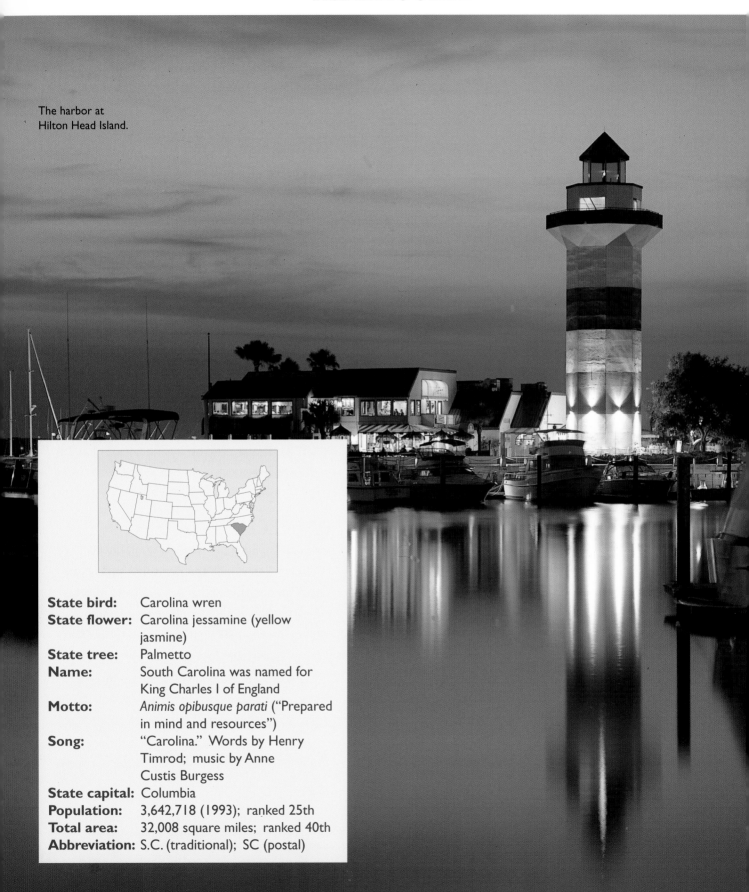

The harbor at
Hilton Head Island.

State bird:	Carolina wren
State flower:	Carolina jessamine (yellow jasmine)
State tree:	Palmetto
Name:	South Carolina was named for King Charles I of England
Motto:	*Animis opibusque parati* ("Prepared in mind and resources")
Song:	"Carolina." Words by Henry Timrod; music by Anne Custis Burgess
State capital:	Columbia
Population:	3,642,718 (1993); ranked 25th
Total area:	32,008 square miles; ranked 40th
Abbreviation:	S.C. (traditional); SC (postal)

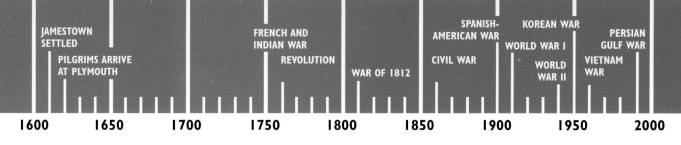

JAMESTOWN SETTLED

PILGRIMS ARRIVE AT PLYMOUTH

FRENCH AND INDIAN WAR

REVOLUTION

WAR OF 1812

SPANISH-AMERICAN WAR

CIVIL WAR

KOREAN WAR

WORLD WAR I

WORLD WAR II

PERSIAN GULF WAR

VIETNAM WAR

1600   1650   1700   1750   1800   1850   1900   1950   2000

South Carolina has many reminders of what the South was like before the Civil War. Buildings erected before the war can still be seen in Charleston, Beaufort, and other cities. There are also many restored plantations in the state. Carefully tended flower gardens are among South Carolina's most beautiful attractions. Visitors to Charleston can visit the Charleston Museum, the oldest museum in the United States. The Old Slave Museum is the oldest museum dedicated to African-American culture.

Eastern South Carolina borders on the Atlantic Ocean. Here, in the region called the Low Country, the land is flat. As you move west, into the Up Country, the land gradually rises to rolling hills and then to mountains. The beautiful Blue Ridge Mountains—in the northwest corner of the state—attract thousands of outdoor enthusiasts each year.

South Carolina is a main producer of textiles; only North Carolina produces more. Peaches are one of the main crops in South Carolina; only California grows more. Other major crops in the state are wheat, tobacco, corn, cotton, and soybeans.

IMPORTANT DATES

• **1521:** Spanish explorer Francisco Gordillo explores the Carolina coast.
• **1670:** The first permanent European settlement in South Carolina is founded at Albemarle Point. It is later moved to present-day Charleston.
• **1788:** On May 23, South Carolina becomes the 8th state.
• **1861:** The Civil War begins when Confederate forces fire on Fort Sumter in Charleston Harbor.
• **1920s:** The boll weevil damages much of South Carolina's cotton crop.
• **1989:** Hurricane Hugo hits the state, causing enormous property damage.

OF SPECIAL INTEREST

• The pirate Blackbeard terrorized the Carolina coast between 1716 and 1718.
• Charleston's Dock Street Theater, which opened in 1736, was the first playhouse in the Thirteen Colonies. It was restored in the 1930s.
• The first steam locomotive used in regular service made its initial run on December 25, 1830. It was called the Best Friend of Charleston.
• The first commercial tea farm in the United States was set up at Summerville in 1890.

Top: An old street in Charleston.
Bottom: State Capitol, in Columbia.

SOUTH DAKOTA

COYOTE STATE; MOUNT RUSHMORE STATE

Mount Rushmore, in the Black Hills, is one of the most famous landmarks in the United States.

State bird:	Ring-necked pheasant
State flower:	American pasqueflower
State tree:	Black Hills (white) spruce
Name:	South Dakota was named for the native Dakota Sioux. *Dakota* means "allies" or "friends"
Motto:	"Under God the people rule"
Song:	"Hail! South Dakota." Words and music by Deecort Hammitt
State capital:	Pierre
Population:	715,392 (1993); ranked 45th
Total area:	77,121 square miles; ranked 17th
Abbreviation:	S. Dak. (traditional); SD (postal)

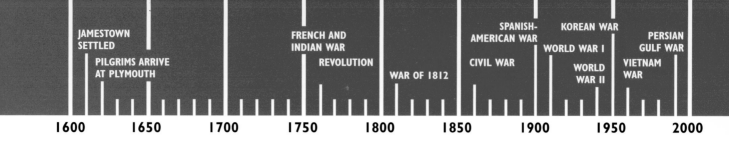

JAMESTOWN SETTLED		FRENCH AND INDIAN WAR				SPANISH-AMERICAN WAR	KOREAN WAR		PERSIAN GULF WAR
PILGRIMS ARRIVE AT PLYMOUTH		REVOLUTION				WORLD WAR I		VIETNAM WAR	
				WAR OF 1812	CIVIL WAR		WORLD WAR II		

1600   1650   1700   1750   1800   1850   1900   1950   2000

The Black Hills, in western South Dakota, have a special place in the state's history. The highest mountains east of the Rockies, they were long sacred to the native Sioux people. In the 1800s, gold was discovered in the mountains, and white settlers rushed to the region. This began a bitter conflict between Native Americans and whites over control of the land.

The Missouri River flows through South Dakota from north to south. East of the river, the landscape is marked by low hills, glacial lakes, and vast stretches of farmland. The Great Plains cover most of the western two thirds of the state. It is here that the barren Badlands can be found. Wind and water have worn the rocks of the Badlands into dramatic, steep cliffs and deep ravines.

South Dakota is primarily a farming state. Its farms and ranches cover about 90 percent of the land. The state is a major producer of beef cattle, sheep, and hogs. South Dakota also ranks high in the production of barley, corn, wheat, oats, rye, hay, soybeans, and other crops. It is also still a leader in the mining of gold.

IMPORTANT DATES

• **c. 1743:** François and Louis Gaultier de Varennes are the first white people to explore the region and claim it for France.
• **1803:** The United States acquires South Dakota from France in the Louisiana Purchase.
• **1817:** Joseph La Framboise establishes the first permanent white settlement, a fur-trading post at present-day Fort Pierre.
• **1874:** Gold is discovered in the Black Hills.
• **1889:** On November 2, South Dakota becomes the 40th state.
• **1890:** U.S. soldiers kill 250 Sioux, including many women and children, at Wounded Knee.
• **1973:** Members of the American Indian Movement occupy the town of Wounded Knee for 70 days.
• **1993:** The worst floods of the century hit the area.

OF SPECIAL INTEREST

• The geographic center of the United States including Alaska and Hawaii is located in Butte County.
• The Homestake Mine is the largest gold mine in the United States. It is located at Lead.
• The largest bison herd in the country is at the Standing Butte Ranch, near Pierre.
• It took 14 years to complete Mount Rushmore National Memorial, where the faces of George Washington, Thomas Jefferson, Abraham Lincoln, and Theodore Roosevelt are carved into the side of a mountain. Construction began in 1927 by sculptor Gutzon Borglum and was completed in 1941.

Top: South Dakota's state flower, the pasqueflower.
Bottom: The dramatic landscape of the Badlands.

TENNESSEE

VOLUNTEER STATE

The sunsphere in Knoxville.

State bird:	Mockingbird
State flower:	Iris
State tree:	Tulip poplar
Name:	The name *Tennessee* comes from the name of a Cherokee village, Tanasi
Motto:	"Agriculture and commerce"
Song:	"The Tennessee Waltz." Words by Pee Wee King; music by Redd Stewart
State capital:	Nashville
Population:	5,098,798 (1993); ranked 17th
Total area:	42,146 square miles; ranked 35th
Abbreviation:	Tenn. (traditional); TN (postal)

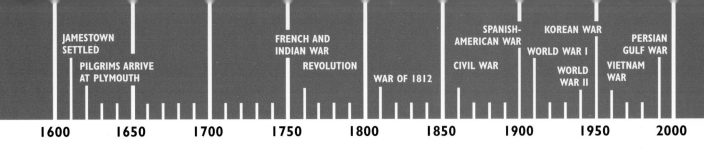

JAMESTOWN SETTLED		FRENCH AND INDIAN WAR				SPANISH-AMERICAN WAR	KOREAN WAR		PERSIAN GULF WAR
PILGRIMS ARRIVE AT PLYMOUTH		REVOLUTION				WORLD WAR I		VIETNAM WAR
			WAR OF 1812	CIVIL WAR		WORLD WAR II	

| 1600 | 1650 | 1700 | 1750 | 1800 | 1850 | 1900 | 1950 | 2000 |

Tennessee is a beautiful mixture of mountains, thick forests, and sparkling lakes and rivers. One of its many attractions is Great Smoky Mountains National Park, with its varied wildlife and rushing streams. The mountains are named for the haze that often hangs over them.

Tennessee's main industries include the making of machines, chemicals, and automobiles. The state's main crops are soybeans and tobacco. Cotton, an important crop in Tennessee's early days, is still grown. Memphis is a major Mississippi River port that began as a cotton market. Nashville, on the Cumberland River, also thrived on cotton in the 1800s. Today, much of the state is covered by rolling farmland, foothills, and pastures. Western Tennessee lies in the vast Mississippi floodplain. It is made up mostly of low rolling hills and wide valley streams.

IMPORTANT DATES

• **1540:** Spanish explorer Hernando de Soto leads the first white expedition into the region.
• **1760:** Daniel Boone explores eastern Tennessee.
• **1796:** On June 1, Tennessee becomes the 16th state.
• **1861:** Tennessee is the last state to leave the Union at the start of the Civil War. (It becomes the first state to be re-admitted, in 1866.)
• **1878:** Yellow fever kills about 5,200 of the 19,600 people living in Memphis.
• **1933:** Congress creates the Tennessee Valley Authority (TVA) to develop the Tennessee River system, control floods, and provide electric power.
• **1968:** Civil rights leader Martin Luther King, Jr., is killed in Memphis.
• **1972:** Construction begins on the Tennessee-Tombigbee Waterway, linking the Tennessee River with the Gulf of Mexico.
• **1982:** The World's Fair is held in Knoxville.

OF SPECIAL INTEREST

• The earliest known people in Tennessee were Native Americans called Mound Builders. They lived in the area about 1,000 years ago.
• Beale Street, in Memphis, is famous as the birthplace of the music style called the blues.
• Nashville is famous as the country music capital of the world.
• Graceland, the home and burial place of Elvis Presley, is located in Memphis.
• Oak Ridge National Laboratory is the largest energy research center in the United States. It had the world's first nuclear reactor in 1943.

Top: Scenic mountains in Gatlinburg.
Bottom: The incline railway at Chattanooga.

TEXAS

LONE STAR STATE

A scenic view of south Texas coastline.

State bird:	Mockingbird
State flower:	Bluebonnet
State tree:	Pecan
Name:	Texas acquired its name from the Caddo word *tejas*, which means "friends" or "allies"
Motto:	"Friendship"
Song:	"Texas, Our Texas." Words by Gladys Yoakum Wright and William J. Marsh; music by William J. Marsh
State capital:	Austin
Population:	18,031,484 (1993); ranked 3rd
Total area:	268,601 square miles; ranked 2nd
Abbreviation:	Tex. (traditional); TX (postal)

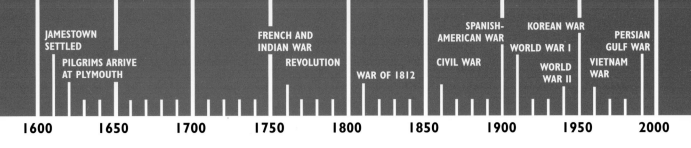

JAMESTOWN SETTLED

PILGRIMS ARRIVE AT PLYMOUTH

FRENCH AND INDIAN WAR

REVOLUTION

WAR OF 1812

SPANISH-AMERICAN WAR

CIVIL WAR

KOREAN WAR

WORLD WAR I

WORLD WAR II

VIETNAM WAR

PERSIAN GULF WAR

1600   1650   1700   1750   1800   1850   1900   1950   2000

Texas is probably best known for cattle ranching and oil wells. But the second-largest state in the nation (after Alaska) has many more attractions to offer. Its southeastern border along the Gulf of Mexico is the site of popular resort spots. The rolling forests of northeast Texas provide many outdoor recreational areas. Texas also has more than 500 festive events each year, more than any other state.

Much of Texas is covered with vast rolling plains. The rich soil of these plains provides fertile farmland, especially along the Rio Grande Valley, in the southern part of the state. The northeastern part of Texas is covered with thick forests. This area is called the Piney Woods. The Rocky Mountains cut across the westernmost part of the state.

Texas has more farms and farmland than any other state. Cotton is the state's leading crop. Fruits and vegetables are also important. Huge cattle and

sheep ranches are scattered over the state's vast prairies and plains. Texas leads the nation in the production of petroleum, and the state has a large aerospace industry.

IMPORTANT DATES
- **1519:** Spanish explorer Alonso Álvarez de Piñeda maps the Texas coast.
- **1682:** Spanish missionaries build the first two missions in Texas near present-day El Paso.
- **1836:** Texas breaks away from Mexico and becomes the independent Republic of Texas.
- **1845:** On December 29, Texas becomes the 28th state.
- **1846:** The first battle of the Mexican War is fought at Palo Alto.
- **1861:** Texas joins the Confederacy in the Civil War.
- **1901:** The great Spindletop oil field is discovered south of Beaumont.
- **1963:** President John F. Kennedy is assassinated in Dallas.
- **1988:** Drought and wind erosion damage more than 2.5 million acres in the state.

OF SPECIAL INTEREST
- The Johnson Space Center, near Houston, is the center of operations for all manned U.S. space flights.
- Texas has the right to divide into five states, according to the terms of an 1845 treaty with the United States.
- Texas covers more area than the states of Illinois, Indiana, Michigan, Ohio, and Wisconsin combined.

Top: The historic Alamo, in San Antonio, site of the famous battle during the Texas Revolution.
Bottom: Texas's state flower, the bluebonnet.

UTAH

BEEHIVE STATE

The Kennecott Copper Mine.

State bird: Sea gull
State flower: Sego lily
State tree: Blue spruce
Name: Utah was named for the Utes, Native Americans who lived in the region before white settlers
Motto: "Industry"
Song: "Utah, We Love Thee." Words and music by Evan Stephans
State capital: Salt Lake City
Population: 1,859,582 (1993); ranked 34th
Total area: 84,904 square miles; ranked 12th
Abbreviation: Ut. (traditional); UT (postal)

JAMESTOWN SETTLED		FRENCH AND INDIAN WAR			SPANISH-AMERICAN WAR	KOREAN WAR		PERSIAN GULF WAR
PILGRIMS ARRIVE AT PLYMOUTH		REVOLUTION				WORLD WAR I		
				CIVIL WAR			VIETNAM WAR
			WAR OF 1812			WORLD WAR II	

| 1600 | 1650 | 1700 | 1750 | 1800 | 1850 | 1900 | 1950 | 2000 |

Utah is famous for its beautiful and varied scenery. Its landscape is made up of colorful, deep canyons, grand, snow-covered mountain peaks, and vast deserts. In some parts of the state, the wind and rain have carved red sandstone into curving arches and high pillars. Utah's Great Salt Lake is the largest natural lake west of the Mississippi River. It is all that remains of what was once a great inland sea. Utah is also famous for its national parks, including Arches, Bryce Canyon, Zion, and Canyonlands.

Utah has three main land regions. The Rocky Mountains cover the northeastern part of the state. The western part of Utah is one of the driest areas of the United States. Most of southern and eastern Utah is covered by high plateaus separated by deep canyons, and valleys.

Large factories in Utah manufacture farm machinery and parts for automobiles and airplanes. The state also has valuable mineral resources, including oil, natural gas, coal, iron ore, copper, gold, and silver. Cattle and sheep graze on Utah's many farms and ranches.

IMPORTANT DATES

• **1776:** Spaniards Silvestre Vélez de Escalante and Francisco Atanasio Dominguez explore the Utah area.
• **1847:** Brigham Young leads the first Mormon pioneers into the Great Salt Lake Valley.
• **1848:** Mexico cedes (gives up) Utah to the United States.
• **1896:** On January 4, Utah becomes the 45th state.
• **1919:** Zion National Park is created.
• **1952:** Large uranium deposits are discovered near Moab.
• **1964:** The Flaming Gorge and Glen Canyon Dams are completed.
• **1983:** Floods cause widespread damage.

OF SPECIAL INTEREST

• The sea gull, Utah's state bird, saved Mormon crops from an invasion of crickets in 1848. Sea Gull Monument, at Salt Lake City, was erected in 1913 to honor the sea gull.
• Great Salt Lake is an inland sea and is one of the natural wonders of the world. The salt concentration in the lake is so high that swimmers float like corks.
• Rainbow Bridge National Monument is the largest-known natural stone bridge in the world. It is located in the Glen Canyon National Recreation Area.
• Vehicles have traveled more than 600 miles per hour at the Bonneville Salt Flats International Speedway, near Wendover.

Top: The sea gull is Utah's state bird.
Bottom: Capitol Reef National Park.

93

VERMONT

GREEN MOUNTAIN STATE

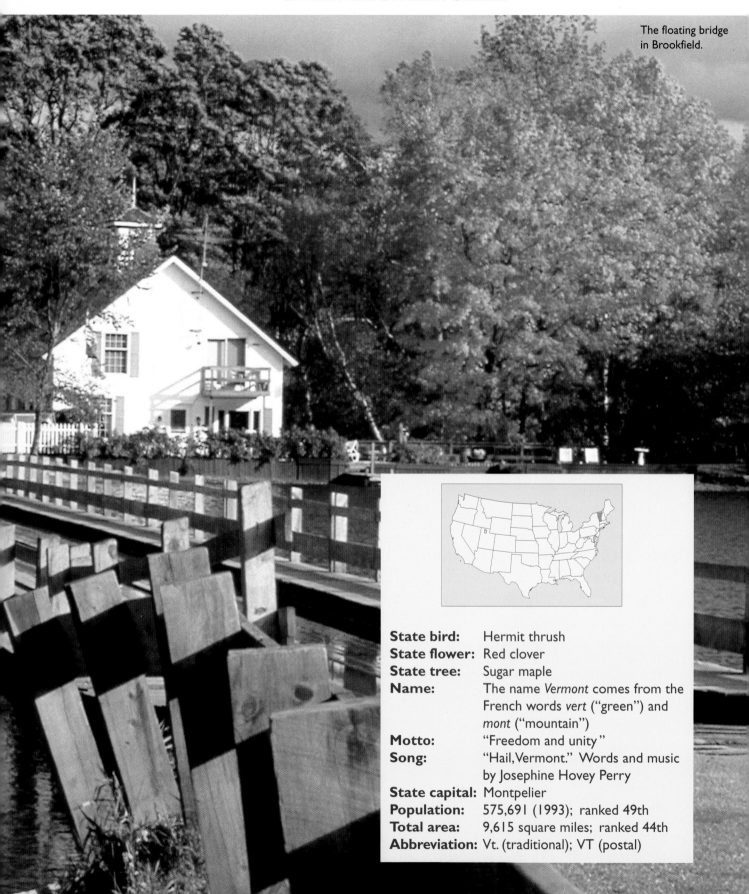

The floating bridge in Brookfield.

State bird:	Hermit thrush
State flower:	Red clover
State tree:	Sugar maple
Name:	The name *Vermont* comes from the French words *vert* ("green") and *mont* ("mountain")
Motto:	"Freedom and unity"
Song:	"Hail, Vermont." Words and music by Josephine Hovey Perry
State capital:	Montpelier
Population:	575,691 (1993); ranked 49th
Total area:	9,615 square miles; ranked 44th
Abbreviation:	Vt. (traditional); VT (postal)

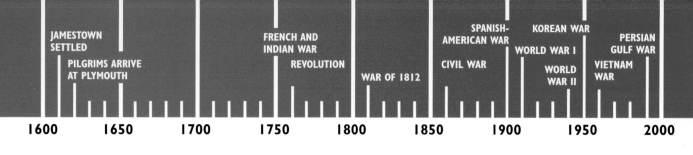

JAMESTOWN SETTLED		FRENCH AND INDIAN WAR			SPANISH-AMERICAN WAR	KOREAN WAR	
PILGRIMS ARRIVE AT PLYMOUTH		REVOLUTION			WORLD WAR I		PERSIAN GULF WAR
			WAR OF 1812	CIVIL WAR		WORLD WAR II	VIETNAM WAR

| 1600 | 1650 | 1700 | 1750 | 1800 | 1850 | 1900 | 1950 | 2000 |

Vermont is famous for its natural beauty and untouched scenery. Forty state parks and 34 state forests attract hikers, campers, cyclists, and sightseers. Each fall, thousands of people come to see the spectacular colors of Vermont's autumn foliage. Long winters and deep mountain snow attract thousands of skiers from around the country to the state's 56 ski resorts.

Vermont's famous Green Mountains run the length of the state. They divide Vermont almost equally into eastern and western sections. In addition, the state has many other mountainous and hilly areas. Forests cover about three fourths of the landscape. The Connecticut River forms Vermont's entire eastern border. Lake Champlain, in the northwestern part of the state, is the largest lake in New England.

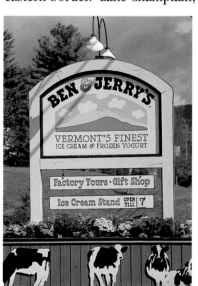

Apples and maple syrup are Vermont's main products. Dairy farming is also important in the state. Vermont's forests supply wood for making paper, furniture, and other wood products. From the state's mountains come granite, marble, and slate that are used as building materials throughout the nation.

IMPORTANT DATES
• **1609:** Samuel de Champlain is probably the first white person to explore Vermont.
• **1724:** Massachusetts establishes Fort Dummer near Brattleboro. It is considered the first permanent white settlement in Vermont.
• **1791:** On March 4, Vermont becomes the 14th state.
• **1864:** Confederate soldiers rob banks in St. Albans and flee to Canada in the northernmost action of the Civil War.
• **1927:** Floods devastate the state.
• **1984:** Madeleine M. Kunin is elected Vermont's first woman governor.

OF SPECIAL INTEREST
• Vermont was the first state to forbid slavery. The issue was included in the state's constitution, signed on July 2, 1777.
• The Concord Academy was the first school whose sole purpose was the training of teachers. It was opened in 1823.
• Vermont has more than 100 covered wooden bridges.
• Two thirds of Vermont's people live in rural areas, more than any other state.
• Vermont is the largest producer of maple syrup in the United States.

Top: A working granite quarry in Barre.
Bottom: Ben & Jerry's ice-cream factory in Waterbury is the state's most popular tourist attraction.

VIRGINIA

OLD DOMINION

A drum corps performs for visitors at Colonial Williamsburg.

State bird: Cardinal

State flower: Flowering dogwood

State tree: Flowering dogwood

Name: Virginia was named for Queen Elizabeth I of England, who was known as the "Virgin Queen"

Motto: *Sic semper tyrannis* ("Thus always to tyrants")

Song: "Carry Me Back to Old Virginia." Words and music by James B. Bland

State capital: Richmond

Population: 6,490,634 (1993); ranked 12th

Total area: 42,777 square miles; ranked 36th

Abbreviation: Va. (traditional); VA (postal)

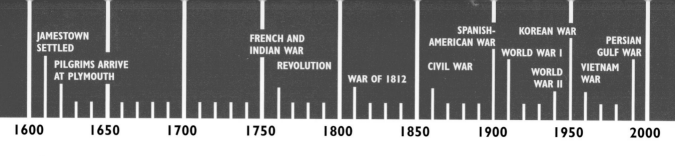

JAMESTOWN SETTLED			FRENCH AND INDIAN WAR			SPANISH-AMERICAN WAR	KOREAN WAR	PERSIAN GULF WAR
PILGRIMS ARRIVE AT PLYMOUTH			REVOLUTION			CIVIL WAR	WORLD WAR I	VIETNAM WAR
				WAR OF 1812			WORLD WAR II	

| 1600 | 1650 | 1700 | 1750 | 1800 | 1850 | 1900 | 1950 | 2000 |

Virginia has an unusually rich history. Jamestown is the site of the first permanent settlement in North America. Restored Colonial Williamsburg was Virginia's capital more than 200 years ago. Yorktown is where the British surrendered to the Americans, ending the Revolutionary War. George Washington's home, Mount Vernon, is near Alexandria. Thomas Jefferson's home, Monticello, is near Charlottesville.

The forested Appalachian Mountains run along Virginia's northeastern border. In some places, the mountains are cut by deep valleys and gorges. East of the Appalachians are the Blue Ridge Mountains. Central Virginia is covered by gently rolling plains, crossed by many rivers and streams. Virginia's Eastern Shore lies on Chesapeake Bay and the Atlantic Ocean.

Virginia is mainly a farming state. Its chief crops are tobacco, peanuts, and corn. The state ranks high in the production of hay, apples, chickens, and turkeys. Virginia is also famous for its hams. Virginia factories produce chemicals, food products, tobacco products, and transportation equipment. Ships for the U.S. Navy and commercial use are built at Virginia shipyards.

IMPORTANT DATES
• **1607:** Jamestown is founded by the Virginia Company of London.
• **1619:** The House of Burgesses, America's first representative legislature, meets at Jamestown.
• **1775:** George Washington, a Virginian, is chosen to lead Patriot forces in the Revolutionary War.
• **1788:** On June 25, Virginia becomes the 10th state.
• **1861-1865:** Virginia joins the Confederacy and is the major battleground of the Civil War.
• **1926:** Historic Williamsburg is restored by John D. Rockefeller, Jr.
• **1964:** The Chesapeake Bay Bridge Tunnel opens, connecting mainland Virginia to the Eastern Shore.
• **1990:** L. Douglas Wilder becomes the first elected African-American U.S. governor.

OF SPECIAL INTEREST
• The only life-size statue of George Washington modeled from life is at the Virginia State Capitol in Richmond. The statue was completed in 1796.
• The largest U.S.-made ocean liner, the S.S. *United States*, was launched from Newport News in 1951.
• Virginia is sometimes called the "mother of presidents" because eight U.S. presidents were born there: Washington, Jefferson, Madison, Monroe, Harrison, Tyler, Taylor, and Wilson.

Top: An aerial view of Mount Vernon, George Washington's home near Alexandria.
Bottom: Virginia's famous Natural Bridge.

97

WASHINGTON

EVERGREEN STATE

Seattle's famous Space Needle dominates the city's nighttime skyline.

State bird: Willow goldfinch
State flower: Western rhododendron
State tree: Western hemlock
Name: Washington was named in honor of President George Washington
Motto: *Al-ki* (a Chinook phrase meaning "By and by")
Song: "Washington, My Home." Words and music by Helen Davis
State capital: Olympia
Population: 5,255,276 (1993); ranked 15th
Total area: 71,302 square miles; ranked 18th
Abbreviation: Wash. (traditional); WA (postal)

JAMESTOWN
SETTLED

PILGRIMS ARRIVE
AT PLYMOUTH

FRENCH AND
INDIAN WAR
REVOLUTION

WAR OF 1812

SPANISH-
AMERICAN WAR

CIVIL WAR

KOREAN WAR

WORLD WAR I

WORLD
WAR II

PERSIAN
GULF WAR

VIETNAM
WAR

1600   1650   1700   1750   1800   1850   1900   1950   2000

Washington is famous for its natural beauty. High mountains rise above evergreen forests and overlook the blue coastal waters of the Pacific. The thick forests of the Olympic Peninsula are draped with vines and moss. Alpine meadows grow on mountain slopes, and there are glaciers among the peaks.

Bays and inlets along Puget Sound provide many excellent harbors. Puget Sound is a large inlet of the Pacific Ocean. The cities of Seattle, Tacoma, and Olympia lie on its shores.

The Cascade Mountains, a chain of mostly dormant volcanoes, divide Washington from north to south. Washington's farmers raise livestock and wheat. The state leads the country in apple production, and is one of the leading growers of flower bulbs. Mild, moist weather makes the western section a rich farming area. Irrigation has turned the drier eastern section into rich farmland, too. Washington's fishing industry is one of the country's largest, and its forests support a large, thriving lumber industry. Commercial airliners and spacecraft are also manufactured in the state.

IMPORTANT DATES
- **1775:** Spanish explorer Bruno de Heceta lands on the Washington coast.
- **1792:** George Vancouver surveys the coast for Great Britain and names Puget Sound.
- **1810:** A British-Canadian trading post is set up near present-day Spokane.
- **1846:** A treaty between the United States and Great Britain establishes Washington's boundaries.
- **1889:** On November 11, Washington becomes the 42nd state.
- **1941:** Grand Coulee Dam is completed.
- **1980:** Mount St. Helens erupts, causing enormous damage.
- **1990:** Seattle and Spokane host the Goodwill Games.

OF SPECIAL INTEREST
- On June 18, 1910, Washington became the first state to celebrate Father's Day. It was the idea of Sonora Louise Smart Dodd of Spokane.
- The first city monorail service in the United States began operating in Seattle in 1962.
- Olympic National Park, on the Olympic Peninsula, protects a temperate rain forest. More than 100 inches of rain fall here each year.
- The greatest annual snowfall in North America occurred at Rainier Paradise Ranger Station. From July 1971 through June 1972, a total of 1,122 inches of snow fell.
- More than 20 Native-American groups lived in the Washington area before Europeans arrived. Many were master woodcarvers who created beautiful masks and totem poles.

Top: Mount Rainier.
Bottom: The carved eye of a Native-American wooden totem.

WEST VIRGINIA

MOUNTAIN STATE

The falls at Blackwater Falls State Park.

State bird: Cardinal
State flower: Rhododendron
State tree: Sugar maple
Name: West Virginia was named for Queen Elizabeth I of England
Motto: *Montani semper liberi* ("Mountaineers are always free")
Song: "The West Virginia Hills." Words by Ellen King; music by H. E. Engle; also, "This Is My West Virginia" and "West Virginia, My Home Sweet Home"
State capital: Charleston
Population: 1,820,137 (1993); ranked 35th
Total area: 24,231 square miles; ranked 41st
Abbreviation: W.Va. (traditional); WV (postal)

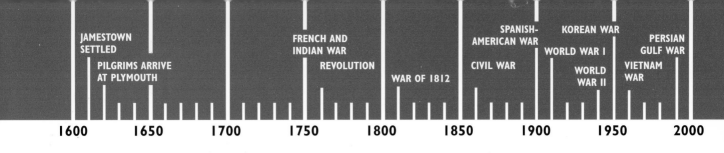

JAMESTOWN SETTLED		FRENCH AND INDIAN WAR			SPANISH-AMERICAN WAR	KOREAN WAR		PERSIAN GULF WAR
PILGRIMS ARRIVE AT PLYMOUTH		REVOLUTION			WORLD WAR I		
			WAR OF 1812		CIVIL WAR	WORLD WAR II	VIETNAM WAR

1600   1650   1700   1750   1800   1850   1900   1950   2000

By the mid-1700s, Virginia had become crowded. Settlers began to cross the Appalachian Mountains in search of cheap land. They found what would become West Virginia, a region of forest-covered mountains, deep gorges, and mineral springs. Today, the state's rugged landscape attracts campers, hunters, and skiers. White Sulphur Springs and Berkeley Springs have been popular health resorts for more than 150 years.

Ranges of the Appalachian Mountains cover the eastern and central sections of the state. The land west of the mountains is covered with hills and narrow valleys. Rivers—the Potomac in the northeast, the Ohio in the west, and the Big Sandy and Tug Fork in the south—form most of the state's borders.

West Virginia is one of the nation's leading

producers of soft coal, chemicals, and steel. The major crops in West Virginia are apples and peaches. Milk, eggs, and honey are other important farm products. Milton and Williamstown are famous glass-making centers.

IMPORTANT DATES

• **1609:** King James I of England grants the area that is now West Virginia to the Virginia colony.
• **1730:** Settlers begin to enter the region.
• **1742:** John P. Salley discovers coal at Racine.
• **1859:** The abolitionist John Brown stages a daring but unsuccessful raid on a federal arsenal at Harpers Ferry.
• **1861:** The western counties of Virginia break away when Virginia leaves the Union at the start of the Civil War.
• **1863:** On June 20, West Virginia becomes the 35th state.
• **1912-1913:** A coal-mine strike leads to bloodshed in the first of many "mine wars" between mine owners and workers who want to form unions.

OF SPECIAL INTEREST

• The first U.S. natural gas well was drilled near Charleston in 1815. A major natural-gas field was discovered in the area in 1965.
• The first free rural mail delivery in the United States began in West Virginia on October 1, 1896.
• West Virginia was the first state to have a sales tax. It went into effect in 1921.
• The world's largest movable radio telescope is located at Green Bank. It began operation in 1962.
• West Virginia is the U.S. manufacturing center of glass marbles. Most of the marble factories are in the Parkersburg area.

Top: The Wheeling suspension bridge at night.
Bottom: The entrance to Greenbriar Resort and White Sulphur Springs.

WISCONSIN

BADGER STATE

An autumn view of the Fall/Eagle River.

State bird: Robin

State flower: Wood violet

State tree: Sugar maple

Name: The name *Wisconsin* may come from the Ojibwa word *ouisconsin*, "the gathering of waters," or from *wishkonsing*, "place of the beavers"

Motto: "Forward"

Song: "On, Wisconsin!" Words by J. S. Hubbard and Charles D. Rosa; music by William T. Purdy

State capital: Madison

Population: 5,037,928 (1993); ranked 18th

Total area: 65,499 square miles; ranked 23rd

Abbreviation: Wis. (traditional); WI (postal)

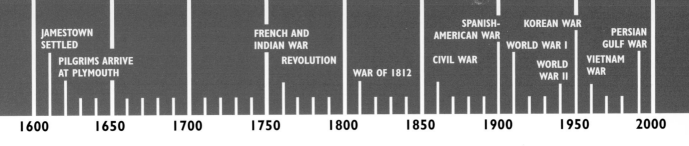

JAMESTOWN SETTLED			FRENCH AND INDIAN WAR		WAR OF 1812	SPANISH-AMERICAN WAR	KOREAN WAR	PERSIAN GULF WAR
	PILGRIMS ARRIVE AT PLYMOUTH		REVOLUTION			CIVIL WAR	WORLD WAR I	VIETNAM WAR
							WORLD WAR II	

| 1600 | 1650 | 1700 | 1750 | 1800 | 1850 | 1900 | 1950 | 2000 |

Wisconsin is nearly surrounded by water. Lake Michigan lies on its eastern border. Lake Superior forms a portion of Wisconsin's northern border. The Mississippi and St. Croix Rivers form the state's western border. This location, on major water routes, has been important to the state. Lakes and rivers brought traders and settlers to the region. Today, they help make Wisconsin a popular vacation spot.

Wisconsin was covered with forests when Europeans first saw it. Except in the north, many of the forests have since been cut down. Farms now cover much of the countryside. There are thousands of small lakes in northern Wisconsin. Much of Wisconsin is covered with rolling plains and pastures.

Wisconsin is dairy land. It is the leading producer of milk in the nation. It provides about a fourth of the nation's butter and more than a third of its cheese. Wisconsin is also a leader in canning vegetables, including peas and sweet corn. The state's factories make electric motors, household appliances, and automobiles. The state also manufactures metal products such as cans, cutlery, and hardware.

IMPORTANT DATES

• **1634:** French explorer Jean Nicolet lands near Green Bay.
• **1665:** Father Claude Allouez founds the first permanent mission at Chequamegon Bay.
• **1673:** Jacques Marquette and Louis Jolliet explore Wisconsin's waterways.
• **1787:** Wisconsin becomes part of the U.S. Northwest Territory.
• **1832:** Black Hawk, a Sauk chief, is defeated in battle and submits to white settlement.
• **1848:** On May 29, Wisconsin becomes the 30th state.
• **1872:** The Wisconsin Dairymen's Association is organized in Watertown.
• **1959:** The St. Lawrence Seaway is completed.
• **1993:** Floods destroy thousands of acres of farmland and cover parts of many towns.

OF SPECIAL INTEREST

• The first lighthouse on Lake Michigan was built in 1837 and stands at Rock Island State Park.
• The world's first hydroelectric plant began operation in Appleton in 1882.
• Malted milk was invented by William Horlick in 1887 in Racine.
• The Dells of the Wisconsin is a gorge filled with odd rock formations carved by the Wisconsin River.

Top: State Capitol, in Madison.
Bottom: Wisconsin's state flower, the wood violet.

WYOMING

EQUALITY STATE

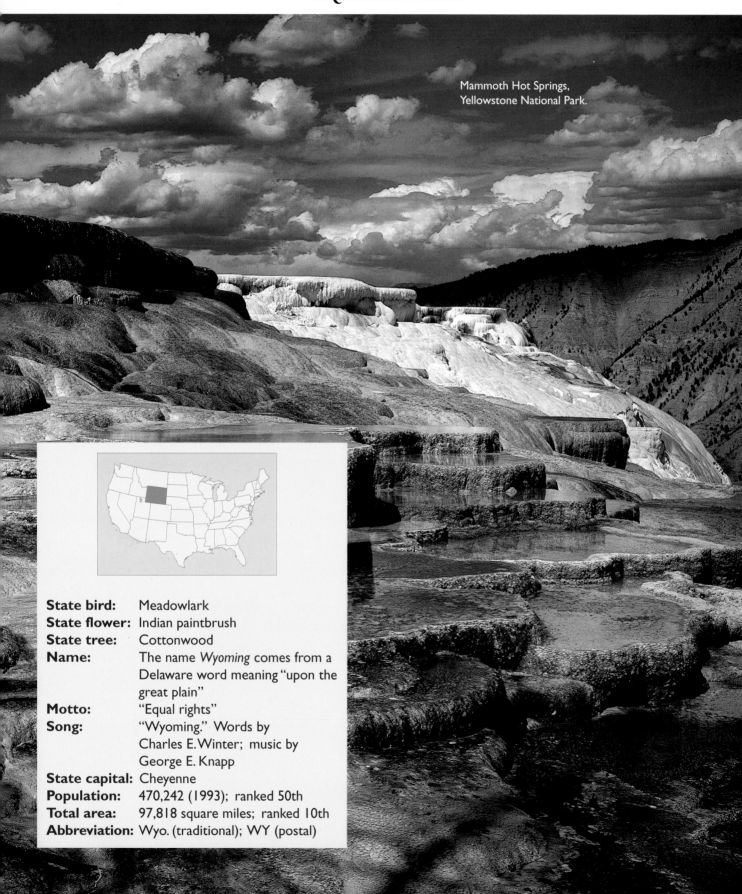

Mammoth Hot Springs,
Yellowstone National Park.

State bird: Meadowlark
State flower: Indian paintbrush
State tree: Cottonwood
Name: The name *Wyoming* comes from a
                    Delaware word meaning "upon the
                    great plain"
Motto: "Equal rights"
Song: "Wyoming." Words by
                    Charles E. Winter; music by
                    George E. Knapp
State capital: Cheyenne
Population: 470,242 (1993); ranked 50th
Total area: 97,818 square miles; ranked 10th
Abbreviation: Wyo. (traditional); WY (postal)

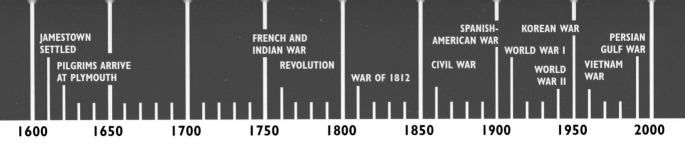

JAMESTOWN SETTLED

PILGRIMS ARRIVE AT PLYMOUTH

FRENCH AND INDIAN WAR

REVOLUTION

WAR OF 1812

SPANISH-AMERICAN WAR

CIVIL WAR

KOREAN WAR

WORLD WAR I

WORLD WAR II

PERSIAN GULF WAR

VIETNAM WAR

1600   1650   1700   1750   1800   1850   1900   1950   2000

Wyoming is famous for its beautiful mountains. The Rocky, Laramie, and Bighorn Mountains cover large areas of the state. The Rocky Mountains provide the backdrop for Yellowstone National Park, the oldest national park in the world. The Wind River and Grand Teton ranges are among the wildest and most spectacular parts of the Rockies. Jackson Hole, a valley famous for its beauty and skiing, lies in the Tetons.

Between the mountain ranges are treeless plains and prairies. There, rugged, lonely towers of rock called buttes jut from the landscape. Devils Tower, in northeastern Wyoming, is a natural column of rock that stands 865 feet high.

About 80 percent of Wyoming's land is used for grazing livestock—mostly cattle. Wyoming has ten times as many cattle as people. The state has large deposits of coal, natural gas, and oil. Wyoming also ranks as a leading state in the mining of uranium. Wyoming produces chemicals, machinery, and food products such as sugar, cheese, and meat. The state's forests provide a large amount of lumber each year.

IMPORTANT DATES

• **1803:** Eastern Wyoming becomes part of the United States in the Louisiana Purchase.
• **c. 1807:** Wilderness traveler John Colter explores the Yellowstone region.
• **1834:** Robert Campbell and William Sublette build the first permanent trading post at present-day Fort Laramie.
• **1890:** On July 10, Wyoming becomes the 44th state.
• **1925:** Nellie Tayloe Ross becomes the governor of Wisconsin—the first woman governor in the United States.
• **1949:** Uranium deposits are discovered in Crook County.
• **1988:** Yellowstone National Park is hard hit by forest fires.

OF SPECIAL INTEREST

• Fossil Butte National Monument is the site of one of the world's largest fossilized fish beds. The fish lived there about 60 million years ago.
• In 1869, the Wyoming Territory passed the first laws in the United States allowing women to vote and hold political office.
• Yellowstone National Park is the world's oldest and the nation's largest national park. It became a national park in 1872.
• Black-footed ferrets were thought to be extinct until a small number were discovered near Meeteese in 1981.
• Cheyenne Frontier Days, a rodeo and Western celebration, has been held annually since 1897.

Top: Shoshone dancers in traditional dress.
Bottom: The world-famous Old Faithful geyser is a main attraction at Yellowstone.

WASHINGTON, D.C.

THE DISTRICT

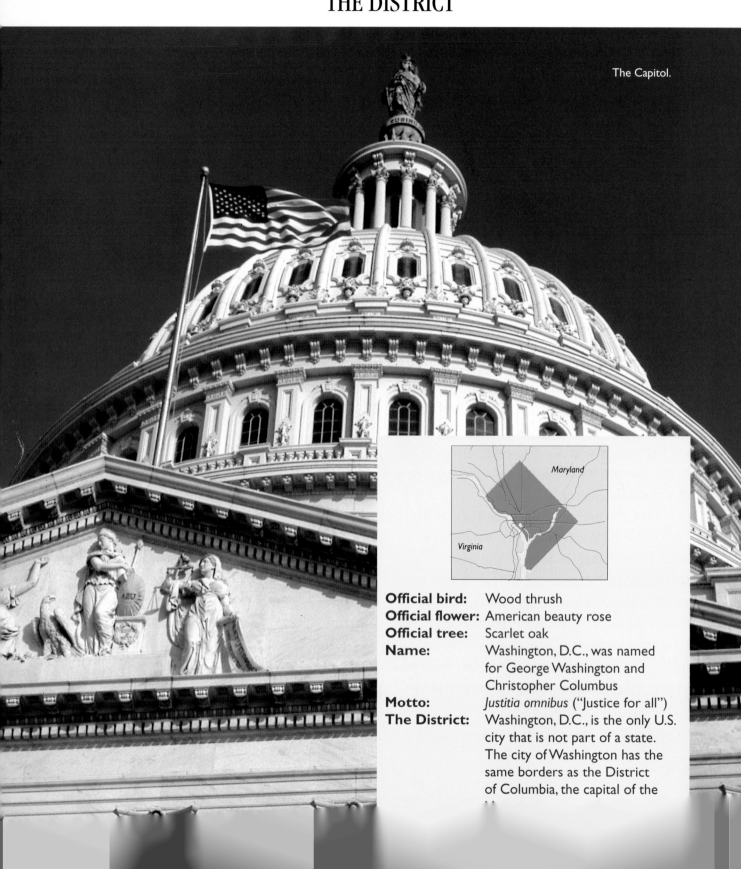

The Capitol.

Maryland

Virginia

Official bird: Wood thrush
Official flower: American beauty rose
Official tree: Scarlet oak
Name: Washington, D.C., was named for George Washington and Christopher Columbus
Motto: *Justitia omnibus* ("Justice for all")
The District: Washington, D.C., is the only U.S. city that is not part of a state. The city of Washington has the same borders as the District of Columbia, the capital of the

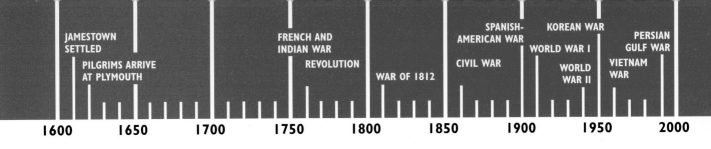

JAMESTOWN SETTLED

PILGRIMS ARRIVE AT PLYMOUTH

FRENCH AND INDIAN WAR

REVOLUTION

WAR OF 1812

SPANISH-AMERICAN WAR

CIVIL WAR

KOREAN WAR

WORLD WAR I

WORLD WAR II

PERSIAN GULF WAR

VIETNAM WAR

1600   1650   1700   1750   1800   1850   1900   1950   2000

The District of Columbia—America's capital city and seat of the U.S. federal government—sits on the northeastern bank of the Potomac River. Today, visitors and area residents alike can enjoy an abundance of historical and cultural activities in the city. Washington, D.C., is home to some of the best museums and libraries in the world, including the massive collections of the Smithsonian Institution. The city is thus a haven for the curious of all ages. Washington, D.C., also boasts many impressive and moving monuments—including the Vietnam Veterans Memorial, the Jefferson Memorial, the Washington Monument, and the Lincoln Memorial—that draw millions of visitors each year. The Capitol building (the center of the nation's legislative branch of government) and the White House (home of the president) are symbols of democracy that are familiar to people all over the globe.

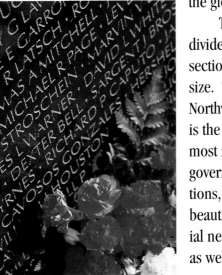

The city is divided into four sections of unequal size. The District's Northwest Quadrant is the area of the most important government attractions, and it has beautiful residential neighborhoods as well.

IMPORTANT DATES

• **1790:** Congress authorizes the establishment of a new federal capital near the Potomac River.
• **1793:** President George Washington lays the cornerstone of the Capitol Building.
• **1800:** Washington, D.C., becomes the permanent home of the U.S. federal government.
• **1814:** The British capture and burn parts of the city—including the Capitol Building and the White House—during the War of 1812.
• **1963:** Martin Luther King, Jr., delivers his famous "I Have a Dream" speech to hundreds of thousands during the civil rights "March on Washington."

OF SPECIAL INTEREST

• The White House was first occupied by John Adams, the second U.S. president, and his wife Abigail. The First Lady hung the family laundry to dry in the unfinished East Room.
• Washington, D.C., originally was to occupy land donated by both Virginia and Maryland. In 1846, the portion given by Virginia was returned.
• The somber and haunting Vietnam Veterans Memorial is a V-shaped granite wall inscribed with the names of the 58,000 Americans who lost their lives in the Vietnam War or who are still missing.
• The Washington Monument, located at the edge of the Reflecting Pool on the Washington Mall, is 555 feet tall. Visitors can enjoy a panoramic view of the nation's capital from the observation deck.

Top: The White House.
Bottom: Some of the 58,000 names engraved on the Vietnam Veterans Memorial.

PUERTO RICO AND THE U.S. TERRITORIES AND POSSESSIONS

The United States holds some degree of jurisdiction—authority or power—over many territories and possessions around the world. A few are large, but most are very small. The majority are in the Pacific; Guam and American Samoa are the best known of these territories. The other most well-known territories—the Commonwealth of Puerto Rico and the U.S. Virgin Islands—are located in the Caribbean Sea.

The relationship between the United States and each territory depends on various factors. Some have close historical, social, and economic ties with the United States, as in the case of Puerto Rico. Other relationships, such as with the Wake Islands in the Pacific, are largely military in nature.

PUERTO RICO
• Puerto Rico, the only U.S. commonwealth, is the most populous of the U.S. territories, with 3,522,037 people living on the island's 3,492 square miles. Another 2.7 million Puerto Ricans live on the U.S. mainland.
• Puerto Rico is represented in the U.S. House of Representatives, but it is self-governing.
• In 1952, Puerto Ricans voted in favor of commonwealth status. Today, nearly half would like Puerto Rico to become the 51st U.S. state—but a nearly equal number are happy with the ways things are. A few others would like Puerto Rico to become an independent country.
• Both English and Spanish are official languages in Puerto Rico.
• San Juan, the capital of Puerto Rico, is one of the world's busiest cruise-ship ports. Its international airport is also a popular transit point for travelers.
• Puerto Rico's diverse and vibrant economy has tourism, manufacturing, and agriculture as its major industries.

Scenic Flamenco Beach in Culebra, Puerto Rico.

JAMESTOWN SETTLED		FRENCH AND INDIAN WAR			SPANISH-AMERICAN WAR	KOREAN WAR		PERSIAN GULF WAR
PILGRIMS ARRIVE AT PLYMOUTH		REVOLUTION				WORLD WAR I		VIETNAM WAR
			WAR OF 1812	CIVIL WAR		WORLD WAR II	

| 1600 | 1650 | 1700 | 1750 | 1800 | 1850 | 1900 | 1950 | 2000 |

GUAM

• Guam is the largest and southernmost of the Mariana Islands. Today, it is an unincorporated U.S. territory and is self-governing.

• The indigenous Guanamanians are a mixture of people of Indonesian, Spanish, and Filipino stock. Ethnically, they are called Chamorros.

• About half of the Guanamanian population of 133,152 were born outside of Guam—mainly in Asia and the United States.

• Because of Guam's strategic location in the Pacific, the United States maintains important air, naval, and port military bases on the island.

• The main industries in Guam are tourism, defense, construction, and banking. The unemployment rate is about 3.8 percent—substantially lower than the U.S. rate of about 5.7 percent.

U.S. VIRGIN ISLANDS

• The three main islands of the U.S. Virgin Islands are St. Croix (population 50,139), St. Thomas (48,166), and St. John (3,504). There are also about 50 small islets and cays.

• Christopher Columbus visited the islands in 1493. Soon thereafter, the Spanish claimed them and, by the late 1500s, had virtually killed off the indigenous population there.

• The United States purchased the territory from Denmark as a defense measure during World War I.

• The U.S. Virgin Islands is called an unincorporated territory. It has a legislature, elected by popular vote, and is headed by an elected governor and lieutenant governor, who serve four-year terms.

• The main industries of the U.S. Virgin Islands are tourism and manufacturing; agriculture is mostly confined to truck produce.

AMERICAN SAMOA

• American Samoa is an incorporated territory consisting of seven islands. Pago Pago, on the island of Tutuila, is the capital.

• Lying deep in the South Pacific, American Samoa is the most southerly of the lands under U.S. sovereignty. Today, it is under the jurisdiction of the Department of the Interior.

• American Samoa has a total area of only 84 square miles and a population of 52,860. More than that number of American Samoans live on the U.S. mainland and in Hawaii.

• American Samoans are largely of Polynesian origin.

• American Samoa relies on the United States for the vast majority of its foreign trade. Tuna products are a major industry in the islands. The government is another important employer.

Top: San Cristobal Fort, Puerto Rico.
Bottom: An aerial view of Guam.

F U R T H E R   R E A D I N G

America the Beautiful (series). Chicago: Childrens Press, 1988.

Ayer, Eleanor. *Our National Monuments.* Brookfield, CT: Millbrook Press, 1992.

Aylesworth, Thomas G. *Kids' World Almanac of the United States.* New York: World Almanac, 1990.

Aylesworth, Thomas G. and Virginia L., *Let's Discover the States* (series). New York: Chelsea House
     Publishers, 1988.

Brandt, Sue R. *Facts about the Fifty States.* Chicago: Watts, 1988.

From Sea to Shining Sea (series). Chicago: Childrens Press, 1993.

Great Cities Library (series). Woodbridge, CT: Blackbirch Press, 1992.

Harrison, James, and Van Zandt, Eleanor, *The Young People's Atlas of the United States.* New York:
     Kingfisher Books, 1992.

Hello U.S.A. (series). Minneapolis: Lerner Publications, 1992.

Hicks, Roger, *The Big Book of America.* Philadelphia: Courage Books, 1995.

James, Ian. *United States.* Chicago: Watts, 1990.

Shapiro, William E. *The Young People's Encyclopedia of the United States.* Brookfield, CT: Millbrook Press,
     1992.

I N D E X